Taking the Tide

Taking the Tide

A MEMOIR

ANTHONY BARBER

A man must make his opportunity,
as oft as find it.

FRANCIS BACON

MICHAEL RUSSELL

For Jean, Louise and Josephine
and my wife Rosemary

First published in Great Britain 1996
by Michael Russell (Publishing) Ltd
Wilby Hall, Wilby, Norwich NR16 2JP

Typeset in Sabon by The Typesetting Bureau
Allen House, East Borough, Wimborne, Dorset
Printed and bound in Great Britain
by Biddles Ltd, Guildford and King's Lynn

ISBN 0 85955 227 6

Contents

CONTENTS

I
Family Matters

My father was a regular visitor to Denmark and it was in Copenhagen, in 1908, that he proposed to Musse Lysberg, a nineteen-year-old fair-haired Danish girl, and brought her back to live in the small town of Hessle near Hull. The Lysberg family at one time controlled the firm of Lysberg Hansen & Therp, which is still one of the finest furniture shops in Copenhagen. In due course the firm passed into other hands, but the family continued to enjoy a comfortable lifestyle.

The contrast between cosmopolitan Copenhagen and life in a small provincial town in the East Riding of Yorkshire was stark. I know from what my mother told me that in those early months she was desperately homesick for her beloved Copenhagen. But she soon adapted to the English way of life, although she never lost her Danish accent. I remember her, in later years, as a passionate defender of all that was British.

One morning in the summer of 1945 my father and I had just finished breakfast. He picked up the *Daily Telegraph* and, after a minute or two, his face turned ashen. I knew something terrible had happened. He continued to stare at the paper, as if in disbelief, and then, without saying a word, he handed the paper over to me. There, on the front page, was the news that my mother had been killed in an air crash. She was flying in a Dakota from Copenhagen to Paris and Air France had released her name to the press before informing the family.

I heard afterwards what had happened. The aircraft had taken off from Copenhagen and then, almost immediately, turned round and landed because of some technical fault. I could well imagine my poor mother, who hated flying, sitting anxiously in that aircraft until the fault was supposedly cured. The aircraft took off again only to plunge into the ground within minutes, killing everyone on board. I remember thinking what a crazy world it was when I came through the war unscathed and she had to die on a simple civil flight from Copenhagen to Paris.

Only a couple of weeks earlier I had been with her in Copenhagen, where she had arranged to stay a little longer before returning home by sea. I was the one who persuaded her to change her plans and fly to Paris to see my brother Noel. She did not want to fly alone. Quite simply, she was frightened. The fact that I persuaded her against her will, and that the flight had ended in disaster, worried me for quite some time.

I went over to Copenhagen to identify what few remnants had been salvaged from the wreckage. What was particularly poignant was that there on the table was the small gold caterpillar brooch which the Irving Parachute Company had given to me, as to all aircrew who successfully baled out during the war. I had given it to her.

Only a few years previously I had flown a Spitfire across the North Sea to photograph the shipyards of Burmeister and Wain in Copenhagen and in the evening I had travelled to London to have dinner with my mother and father. I can still remember her surprise when I produced a photograph of the centre of Copenhagen taken at 30,000 feet earlier that same day.

My father, John, came from a very different background. There were six children in the family, two boys and four girls. They were strictly brought up by their father, Benjamin Barber, in the small Derbyshire village of Bradwell. Benjamin, who had a few acres of land, was a Wesleyan-Methodist lay preacher who was said never to have worked, but who spent the whole of his life travelling the Derbyshire hills and preaching the Gospel.

Whenever he was short of money he would sell off another parcel of land, and maybe the Good Lord did take care of him for it was said that he had just disposed of his last field when he died. Certainly there was nothing left for the family and so my father, who had been articled to a solicitor in Sheffield, had to abandon the law and earn his living.

Many years later, when I had grown up, I remember him as being exceptionally well read, a good after-dinner speaker and a stickler for the correct use of the English language. Perhaps because in his youth he had had his fill of Methodist preaching, in later years he enjoyed somewhat more than his fair share of Highland Queen. When my brother Noel produced one of his best-selling novels,

Tanamera, it was easy to recognise one of the central characters, 'Jack', as being our father.

I still have a vivid recollection of the circumstances which led to the end of my father's working days. I had not been in the House of Commons for long when he sought my advice. He was managing director of a medium-sized private limited company. He had no stake in the company which was owned by the chairman. The Investigation Branch of the Inland Revenue suspected the chairman of having charged to the company a substantial item of purely personal expenditure. I told my father there was only one sensible course and that was to tell the Revenue all he knew. He did just that, with consequences which are hard to believe these days. He had no contract of employment, having naively assumed that as he was largely responsible for making the chairman a wealthy man, he would be properly looked after on retirement. It was not to be.

The chairman, who had to pay substantial penalties to the Inland Revenue, was furious with my father for disclosing the truth and sacked him without a penny – no ex gratia payment and no pension. Furthermore, he was living in a company house and, with indecent haste, he was served with a notice to quit. He had no redress but, typically, he accepted the position philosophically.

Soon afterwards he married his ex-secretary, Kathleen, who later qualified as a schoolteacher. They had one daughter, my half-sister Jane. We all love Jane and, with the passage of time, we now see much more of her.

My two brothers, Noel and Kenneth, were both born before the First World War. I arrived some ten years later and I suppose that I must have been something of an afterthought. I have sometimes wondered whether I would have been around at all if an incident at the beginning of the Great War had turned out differently. It was in the summer of 1914, six years before I was born, and my father and mother, with their two young sons, were spending a holiday in Denmark. Although there was much talk of war it was not until 4 August when war was declared that they hurriedly arranged to return to England on a Danish ship, the *Vicaria*. They were crossing the North Sea when the *Vicaria* was intercepted by two German destroyers, boarded and escorted to Hamburg. Probably because the boat was Danish and Denmark was neutral she was eventually permitted to proceed and so, several days later, she finally arrived at Hull.

I have said that Noel and Kenneth were some ten years older than I. Such a difference in age now seems to be of little significance but it made all the difference in my younger days. I suppose that it was not until I came home after the war that I looked upon them as companions rather than as elder brothers. Because Noel was by far the most flamboyant of the three of us there is more to say about him. But, despite his prolific output of books of one sort or another, the most intellectual of the three of us was undoubtedly Kenneth, a man with a wide literary appreciation. He rose steadily up the ladder in the Midland Bank and then, having decided that a traditional banking career was not for him, he was appointed the bank's Secretary – a position he enjoyed until he retired many years ago. His work with the bank left him with enough time to write many short stories for the old London *Evening News* and various other publications. My thanks go to him for helping me to knock these memoirs into what is, I hope, a readable shape.

Noel was a great character. His first job in journalism was as a young reporter on a local weekly newspaper. After only one year's experience he had the audacity to submit to Pitmans a book entitled *Newspaper Reporting* – which they published. In due course he became chief foreign correspondent of the *Daily Mail*. Wherever there was trouble, he was there – Morocco, Indo-China, Syria, Algiers. In 1954 he was stabbed by a terrorist while reporting anti-French riots in Casablanca. Two years later he was shot in the head by a Russian sentry in Budapest. I well remember this last incident. His wife telephoned me in desperation, having just received the news that he was in hospital, and I walked straight over to the Foreign Office where I saw some official who was dealing with the Hungarian uprising. He calmly told me that Noel should not have been in Budapest. I restrained myself.

To me the most interesting aspect of Noel's career is not his adventures as a foreign correspondent, nor the thirty odd non-fiction books which he wrote, but the fact that he wrote his first novel at the age of seventy. He then produced one novel a year until he died and every one was a best seller.

Such was my family background. Every year before the war we spent long summer holidays in Copenhagen and on the Danish island of Bornholm in the Baltic. Happy memories of those summers abound. They were glorious days, every day was sunny, or so I remember them. Even the fact that my first young love did not return my affections does not detract from those boyhood memories. All my days were spent with Danish children and the only means of communicating was to speak Danish. I never had a lesson nor did I ever read or write Danish, but I very soon became fluent in the language of children (the limited vocabulary of which included all those 'rude' words which little boys pick up).

My education was uneventful – a small kindergarten, a local private school and then a boarder at Retford Grammar School. I cannot pretend that I enjoyed school very much but there is no doubt that Retford Grammar School, founded by Edward VI in 1551, gave me a first-class education. It may not have had the cachet of the famous names but, for a boy from a middle-class family, attendance at a good grammar school provided just as sound a preparation for entry into this turbulent world. Soon after leaving school I was articled to a solicitor. And then came the war.

2

The Fall of France

It was in the early afternoon of Sunday, 25 January 1942 that I baled out of my Spitfire at 15,000 feet, did a free fall for a while to make sure that I did not get entangled with the tail of the aircraft, and then floated gently down towards Mont-St-Michel. Anyone who has ever seen Mont-St-Michel will understand that what was uppermost in my mind in those minutes as I descended closer and closer to earth was not the thought of being taken prisoner by the enemy but of crashing onto the rooftops or, even worse, hitting the abbey spire.

The aircraft spiralled down into the sea, so what the Germans never knew was that it was no ordinary Spitfire. It had no guns and no radio. But more of that later. What did puzzle them was that I was not in Air Force blue, but was wearing the khaki uniform of an Army lieutenant with RAF pilot's wings.

To explain the reason for the Army uniform, I must go back to the summer of 1939. I was eighteen years old and, difficult though it now is to believe, before receiving any training I was commissioned in the local Territorial regiment. I was to have command of some fifty men who comprised my troop and, come the autumn, we were in France as part of the British Expeditionary Force. Most of the men were coal miners from the small mining village of Denaby in the West Riding of Yorkshire. They seemed as fine a group of men as anyone could wish for, and proved to be so when the real war started in 1940.

How things have changed in my lifetime. Here were fifty men, almost all of them older than I was and some of them veterans of the First World War, under the command of an eighteen-year-old youth who had never served in the ranks. The men accepted the position without resentment and I saw nothing particularly strange in the situation.

Within a week of the declaration of war, the Regiment was

assembled on Thursley Heath in Surrey. Just before we embarked
for France, the CO had us all lined up for a pep talk. In particular,
he stressed the importance of setting a good example to the French.
He referred to the temptations in a foreign country and then uttered
some words which did not quite convey the meaning he intended: 'I
expect that from time to time you will be meeting French ladies.
When you do, I want you to treat them just as you would treat your
own womenfolk at home.' The troops roared their approval.

Before the month was out we sailed for Normandy. The other
ranks spent the night on deck. The officers shared the cabins. Some
episodes in life stand out and I remember quite vividly lying awake
and listening to the ribald songs of the men with whom I was to
share the next few months, and wondering what the future held for
all of us. I do not think that any of us thought it remotely possible that, at the end of those few months, we would be part of a
defeated army pushed by the enemy into the sea.

When we arrived in France, we were stationed at a town called
Seclin. Morale was high and, with the passage of time, my confidence was growing and I had developed excellent relations with
the men in my troop. Because it was a Territorial regiment, I knew
most of the officers. There was a great spirit of camaraderie and
I was enjoying life as a young subaltern. I was personally very
well organised. I had managed to get myself billeted with the local
butcher (with obvious advantages) and, from some new Reservists
who had joined us, I selected as my batman a man who claimed he
had previously been batman to General Ironside. He would wake
me with a cup of tea in the very early hours of the morning, for the
routine was that I had to inspect all four gun sites before first light.
This was the period of the 'phoney war' and there were frequent
evening trips in the 15 cwt truck to Lille where there was much to
open the eyes of Second Lieutenant Barber.

The ingenuity of the troops knew no bounds. To give just one
instance. How to keep warm on the gun sites when the powers that
be provided no fuel? The answer came from one of the gun crews
who were sited near a railway track on which passed a succession
of slow goods trains. The troops would take turns in standing by
the line and, whenever a train approached, they would shout to the
engine driver: 'Charbon, charbon!' We were never short of coal.

My troop seemed to have a continual succession of visitors.
I remember two in particular. There was Brigadier Sir Isidore

Salmon (of Salmon and Gluckstein) who had the imposing title of 'Honorary Catering Adviser to The British Expeditionary Force'. He was a pleasant enough man and asked all the obvious questions, but I do not recall any significant improvement in the quality of the catering.

Another visitor was the Duke of Gloucester. As he arrived at the gun site, I called the crew to attention. I understood that it was then for the Duke to tell me to stand the men at ease. More and more time passed and, as the leisurely talk continued, the men continued to stand to attention. I suppose that if I had had little more experience and confidence, I would have asked the Duke for permission to stand them at ease. What the men had to say afterwards about the Duke does not bear repetition.

One of my duties was to censor all the men's outgoing mail. It is hard to believe in this day and age but it was accepted by the troops without demur and, judging by the explicit language in their letters to their wives and girlfriends, they were not in the least inhibited by the arrangement. For me, it was just one more eye-opener.

So there I was, completely unconcerned about any possible dangers which might lie ahead. The truth is that I was thoroughly enjoying myself, perhaps partly because I was with brother officers who came from the same part of Yorkshire and, by and large, the same sort of background. Then there were those fifty NCOs and gunners. I had developed not only admiration for the uncomplaining way in which they took everything in their stride, but also a real affection for them.

It was while I was enjoying this happy state of affairs that, like a bolt from the blue, I was told that I was being sent to a transit depot near Nantes to await a further posting. Apparently we were one officer over strength and, as I was the youngest, I was the one who had to go. I spent the next few weeks kicking my heels at the transit depot, and those weeks must surely rank as among the most miserable I can remember.

I wrote to the CO, asking whether he would bear me in mind in the event of the Regiment being short of a subaltern at any time in the future. How or why it happened I do not know, but after a month or so I was back with the Regiment and once again in command of my old troop.

I suppose that we were a bit of a Fred Karno's army. At any rate that must have been the view of those on high, for our

Commanding Officer and several other officers, including my battery commander, were posted back to England and replaced by Regulars. Our new CO was a colonel from the RHA, Colonel Revell-Smith, and his very appearance put the fear of God in me. Our new battery commander was Major Adrian Matthews. I have to admit that the Regular officers who took command did knock us into some sort of shape.

The German Army crossed into Belgium on 10 May 1940. The moment the first shell fell, our Lieutenant Quartermaster, who was responsible for the whole of the Regiment's equipment and stores, went almost wild with relief. 'That's what I've been waiting for all these months. Now I can account for every single item that's missing.'

I have often reflected how bizarre it was that, only a few years before the Germans struck, I had been marching through Bavaria with the Hitler Youth. It came about in this way. A close friend of my mother was another Dane who was married to a German with the unusual name of Malcomes. Their son, Sven, was about my age. I had just left school and in order to give myself time to consider my future, I went to stay with the Malcomes and learned to speak German. Those few months in Germany proved to be invaluable when, later in the war, I found myself with sufficient knowledge of German to escape from a prison camp in Poland and travel by train back through Germany.

Neither Mr nor Mrs Malcomes had any time for the Nazis, but Mr Malcomes knew that if he spoke out he would almost certainly lose his job as managing director of a substantial company in the Ruhr. Who am I to say that he should have had more courage? After all, this was the year in which Lloyd George was hailing Hitler as a great and wonderful leader. Sven had really no alternative but to join the Hitler Youth if he was to have any chance of making progress, and so it happened that, for a modest payment, I was invited to join Sven's Hitler Youth group for a ten-day 'tour' down to Bavaria.

I had only a superficial idea of the situation in Germany, and at first I found the German boys I was mixing with not unlike any other boys. But the better I got to know them the more I became aware of something unpleasant about the attitude of many of them. It was not just that they were arrogant. They were cruelly unsympathetic about one of their number who was clearly something of a weakling and had difficulty in keeping up with the pace of the marching. There was a minor incident when they started jeering at some cleric at a railway station. Then there were not infrequent references to Jews.

I stayed on in Germany for another couple of months or so and was very relieved to get back to a more wholesome environment in good old England. If I was politically naive when I arrived in Germany, I was much wiser when I left. Anyway, for a boy of sixteen it was an interesting experience.

To revert to the events of May 1940. When the Germans invaded Belgium, the Regiment moved up to meet them and I remember how proud we all felt as we travelled through the towns and villages on the receiving end of cheering crowds of Belgians who lined the streets. As a lowly troop commander I had no idea of our tactics. At nineteen I had complete confidence in my superiors. It seemed perfectly natural to me that I should simply carry out the orders I was given, and my four gun crews never questioned the orders I gave them. We were all brimful of confidence. We were on our way to give the Germans a bloody nose and to 'hang out the washing on the Siegfried Line'.

But it was not to be. Within a couple of weeks we were in retreat. No more cheering crowds lining the streets, but instead small groups of mainly older men and women watching us in silence with expressions of incomprehension and almost disbelief. They wore the same expressions of hopelessness and fear which I was to see on the faces of German civilians some years later when I was being held by the Russians during their final assault on Berlin.

Only gradually did it dawn on me that we were engaged in a retreat of massive proportions. As we withdrew I got word that a trainload of NAAFI goods was standing at a nearby railway terminal. The area was about to be evacuated, so I immediately sent off two men in a 15 cwt truck to get what they could. They had strict orders to get back quickly as we were soon to move on. The truck came back loaded with tinned food and other produce including a case of whisky and, as a gesture to their troop commander, a carton of 5,000 of my favourite cigarettes – Players No. 3.

Just outside the coastal resort of La Panne I was told to halt my troop and to await further orders. Realising that in all probability there were going to be demanding times ahead, it seemed to me to be only sensible to snatch a short rest. I had had much less sleep than the men and anyway there was nothing in particular for me to do. So I lay down in the back of a 30 cwt truck with instructions that I should be woken in half an hour – or before then if there were any developments. The next thing I knew was being roused by an absolutely furious Commanding Officer. What on earth did I think I was doing sleeping in the middle of the day? He was in no mood to accept an explanation so, however unfair, the only thing to do was to accept the rebuke. The suggestion that I was failing in my duty was hard to take, but the men in my troop knew the truth and understood.

Soon we were on the move again, through La Panne and on to the beach where a major evacuation was taking place. We set up our Bofors anti-aircraft guns and at times there seemed to be almost endless waves of attacking German aircraft. I remember in particular the screech of the Stuka dive bombers. We did our best to make it more difficult for them to strafe the troops on the beach – not to mention ourselves.

I was told that we were to stay where we were until the evacuation was complete. It was then that I began to realise that, if we were to be the last to leave, there was a real possibility that we might not get away. The same thoughts must have occurred to the men but none of them showed the slightest sign of panic.

After some days we were running short of ammunition and had to ration our firing. Only very occasionally did we see a British aircraft and inevitably the question was asked, 'Where's the bloody RAF?' We did not know then that the RAF was conserving its force for home defence. Meanwhile, as the evacuation gathered pace there was absolute chaos on the approaches to the beach. The Belgian Army had capitulated and there were abandoned vehicles everywhere blocking the roads and preventing ambulances from getting through. But my abiding recollection is of the discipline of the British troops as they waited patiently for their turn to be evacuated.

Eventually, as the Germans got closer, those members of the battery whose presence was no longer essential were ordered to join the evacuation. Unhappily, many of them were aboard a ship (which I think was called the SS *Gracie Fields*) when she was hit and sunk by dive bombers. Those of us who remained continued to man the guns until the evacuation was complete. Our last act at La Panne was to immobilise the guns so that they would be useless to the advancing enemy. We were told to make our way to Dunkirk which was only a few miles west of La Panne. We could see the pall of smoke from the burning oil tanks there. In the event, we never made it. The Germans were moving very fast and we were cut off. We came across a large rowing boat and headed out to sea.

Twenty-three years later, when I was the MP for Doncaster, a letter appeared in the local weekly newspaper. With some hesitation, I have decided to reproduce it – it is after all part of the story. It was from a gunner in my troop who declared himself to be a Labour voter. After referring to the retreat from Brussels, he continued:

> I was with him [Mr Barber] on the night of May 31 and the morning of June 1, 1940. During those last hours on the beaches he was ordering guns and lorries to be immobilised in accordance with GHQ orders.
>
> When this had been done two trucks which had been left intact were used to pick up the wounded on the beaches, and Mr Barber was seeing to this himself. Eventually we found a rowing boat which was loaded up with wounded and a few fit men were told to row out to HMS *Salamander*, where the wounded were taken aboard and made as comfortable as possible.
>
> I remember making inquiries about Mr Barber while on the *Salamander* and was told he and a soldier had taken the rowing boat back to fetch some men left on the beaches, among them Major Matthews, our battery major.

In only a few months Colonel Revell-Smith, our CO, and Major Matthews, our battery commander, had transformed a group of part-time soldiers into something approaching professionals. Colonel Revell-Smith was awarded the DSO and Major Matthews the MC.

I was just nineteen when we went to France and I was still nineteen when we landed at Dover. But I was much more than eight months older.

After the fall of France the Regiment was eventually assembled in Dorset. We had returned to England with no guns, no transport and, indeed, no equipment of any kind. You would have thought that morale would have been at rock-bottom. Maybe it was among some of those in senior positions who were now facing up to the enormity of the task which lay ahead; but my recollection is that those of us in more lowly positions were in remarkably good heart. We were soon provided with commandeered transport and then with a few Bofors guns and tractors which we drove back and forth along the South Coast. I have often wondered whether the local inhabitants realised that in those early days after Dunkirk it was the same few anti-aircraft guns which kept on passing by.

Meanwhile, we were beginning to enjoy life with nightly visits to Bournemouth. I remember particularly a young receptionist at the Branksome Towers Hotel. Then one night I was driving back to base with my battery captain in the passenger seat. It was a pitch black night and it was difficult to see the road signs because of the blackout. Unwittingly, I was driving the wrong way down a one way street. Worse, I did not see a policeman standing in the middle of the road with his back to me. I found out later that he was standing there in order to stop an oncoming car whose head-lights were too bright. I jammed on my brakes as hard as I could but just – only just – failed to avoid hitting him. He fell to the ground in front of the oncoming car which also just touched him. Miraculously he was not badly hurt and, without waiting for an ambulance, I drove him straight to hospital.

As a budding lawyer, I realised that – putting it mildly – things did not look good for me. It required no imagination to visualise the case for the prosecution:

'The accused had been spending the whole evening out on the town. He was driving a commandeered car other than on official business. He carelessly drove the wrong way down a one way street. He hit a police constable who was standing in the middle of the road.'. . .

Fortunately, because I knew that I was to drive my battery captain back to base, I was completely sober.

Some days later the Chief Constable sent for me. I arrived in trepidation and feared the worse. I need not recount the details of the interview, merely that the Chief Constable told me that no further action was to be taken. I called to see the policeman just before he left hospital. His only problem was a slight stiff neck which he was told would gradually right itself. But for the time being he could only turn his head properly in one direction. When I mentioned this to my battery captain, he said somewhat callously 'They could always put him back on a one way street.'

3
Photographic Reconnaissance

After Dunkirk it was clear that the British Army had ahead of it a long period of retrenchment before it would be ready for offensive action on the scale required to win the war. It was not an appealing prospect. During the Battle of Britain my troop had been deployed at Gatwick and I had seen much of the action by the RAF over that area of the South of England. I was not alone among men of my age in being envious of those who flew. Maybe it was just a youthful quest for adventure and action but, whatever it was, I determined that somehow or other I would become a pilot.

There was no question of my being able to relinquish my Army commission and transfer to the RAF, but I had heard that some Army officers were seconded to the Air Force for certain specific duties. I need not detail how I set about contriving the change. Suffice it to say that I put away my spectacles, stopped smoking, passed a superficial medical, was accepted and before the year was out was flying solo.

There was the usual succession of training aircraft, then Hurricanes and Mustangs. Finally I was posted to Old Sarum to fly Lysanders. I was never told what I was being trained for but, because of the Lysander's very short take off and landing, they were sometimes used for taking agents in and out of enemy-occupied territory. In any event I was soon to move on.

At RAF Benson, in Oxfordshire, there was based the Photographic Reconnaissance Unit, or PRU, flying specially adapted Spitfires without guns or radio which could stay up for more than five hours and fly deep into enemy territory. Before I explain how I came to join the unit, I should say that my modest involvement with PRU left me with lasting admiration for the men who conceived and developed what must surely rank as one of the most remarkable outfits of the wartime RAF.

One of those men was Sidney Cotton, whose determination and

unorthodox approach created what became known as 'Cotton's Circus', the precursor of PRU. To gauge the character of the man, consider this story taken from Andrew Brookes's book, *Photo Reconnaissance*. He tells how in September 1939 the First Sea Lord was pressing Air Marshal Sir Richard Peck, the Director General of Operations, for photographs of the Dutch coast between Flushing and Ymuiden where a German force was reported to be concentrating.

Cotton, who at that time was still a civilian, was asked for his advice as to how to overcome an apparently insurmountable technical problem. Eventually the frustrated Cotton told the meeting that if the RAF would lend him a Blenheim, he would get the pictures straight away. Not surprisingly, the possibility of a civilian being shot down in an RAF aircraft was unacceptable. Cotton left Whitehall a disappointed man. He said later: 'I went back to my office high above St James's Square and stared dejectedly out of the window, over the hills to the twin towers of the old Crystal Palace and beyond. . . . Then I looked again at the blue sky and the clouds. It was one of those days when anyone who loves flying longs to get airborne. Why not? Why not take the Lockheed and go and get the pictures now?'

Before long Cotton was crossing the Kent coast in his civil aircraft bound for the mouth of the Scheldt. The cameras turned over both Flushing and Ymuiden, and then it was back across the North Sea to Farnborough. The School of Photography worked all night developing and printing so that Cotton could be in Peck's office at 10 a.m. the next morning with an album of enlargements in his briefcase.

Peck opened the meeting and the talk proceeded much as it had done the day before. After half an hour Cotton produced the album. 'Is this the sort of thing you want?' he asked. Peck examined each print critically and was full of praise for the photography. The places were clearly marked with the respective place-names, but it was taken for granted that they were of pre-war origin.

'These are first class,' said Peck, handing the album round, 'but we wouldn't expect this sort of quality in wartime.' Cotton said nothing. Then someone asked when the pictures were taken, and Cotton replied: 'At three-fifteen yesterday.' The next day the Chief of the Air Staff asked Cotton to take charge of photographic reconnaissance in the RAF.

Later on the Commanding Officer of PRU was Wing Commander Geoffrey Tuttle, and I had been told that he had the authority to select any pilot he wanted. I somehow managed to get an introduction to one of the flight commanders, Flight Lieutenant Neil Wheeler. Unfortunately he was based at St Eval in Cornwall. I had no car, so there was only one thing to do. I flew a Lysander down to St Eval and, with some trepidation, asked to see Flight Lieutenant Wheeler.

'Nebby' Wheeler (who is now a retired Air Chief Marshal) remembers the occasion well. He says that he was somewhat surprised at the uninvited arrival of a young flying officer who asked him what the chances were of joining the unit. We had quite a long talk and he was obviously weighing me up. I sensed that I was making progress when, to my amazement, he said 'I've never flown a Lysander. If you'll let me fly it for half an hour I will recommend you to Wing Commander Tuttle.' My last words to him before he took off were to the effect, 'Please do be careful. I'll get into terrible trouble if you damage it.' His log book shows that he took off at 11.25 on 9 October 1941. He handed back the aircraft intact!

So I joined PRU and soon after made my first flight in that most beautiful of all aircraft, the Spitfire. I have already mentioned that these particular aircraft had no guns and no radio. The purpose was to save both weight and space in order to carry both the cameras and as much fuel, oil and oxygen as possible to maximise the time the aircraft could remain airborne. So, whereas the basic fighter Spitfire had 85 gallons of fuel, the PRU Spitfire carried 220. An additional reason for removing the radio was, we were told, that the lack of a radio mast gave the aircraft another 10 mph which was a distinct advantage when you were completely unarmed and being chased by Messerschmitts deep in enemy territory. The optimum height for the longer sorties was 30,000 feet, and at that height the cold was intense. Not only was there no cockpit heating until later, but in those days there was no pressurisation.

The intense cold coupled with the lack of pressurisation had one or two indelicate consequences. The higher you flew the lower the pressure in the atmosphere, so the need to equalise the high pressure inside the body with the low pressure outside the body was a hygienic challenge. Then there was the very real problem of what to do if you wanted to make yourself comfortable in the other respect.

A tube strapped to the leg was tried but was no use because the contents froze. So you just had to do the best you could.

The navigation was primitive in the extreme. With no radio, no navigator and unreliable weather forecasts, you simply plotted your track and set your course, climbed to 30,000 feet, hung on to your map of Europe and prayed that when there was a break in the cloud you might recognise some configuration of railway lines or a bend in a river which would enable you to check your position. If you were over ten-tenths cloud, there was simply nothing you could do but press on and hope for the best. You could not go down below the clouds, first because your fuel consumption increased the lower you descended and, second, because being unarmed you would stand no chance against enemy fighters attacking from above.

The lack of radio or of any kind of navigation facilities other than a simple map made long flights over cloud particularly hazardous. Occasionally you would be over cloud for the whole of the outward and return journeys. And, with cross winds of up to 100 mph, you frequently had little idea where you were when you finally broke through the cloud – hopefully somewhere over Britain where the land was reasonably flat and low. If you were not able to determine your position you landed where you could. On one occasion, as dusk was descending and with no airfield in sight, I chose what seemed in the half light to be a suitable large field, only to find out almost immediately on touching down that it was dotted with large poles to prevent the enemy from landing. The aircraft was a complete write-off, but the photographs were safe.

There was one other consequence of having no radio. If that single Rolls-Royce engine failed, for instance over the North Sea, you had no means of alerting anyone or giving your position, and you knew that, even if you ditched safely in the sea, there would be no action by the Air-Sea Rescue Services. Later on the unit was equipped with Mosquitoes with twin engines, radio and navigator. But I am pleased that it was a Spitfire that I flew in those early days.

Perhaps I can digress here to mention that, many years later, I was invited to chair an appeal to mark the fiftieth anniversary of the Battle of Britain. I suppose it was inevitable that in most of the appeal material we should have given pride of place to the Spitfire whereas in fact the principal aircraft in the Battle of Britain was the Hurricane and, in my view, the real heroes of the war in the air were the bomber crews. Many people know that over 55,000 aircrew in Bomber Command were killed on operations, but it is less well known that of every 100 aircrew in the Command between 1939 and 1945 only 24 emerged unscathed, the others being killed, wounded or taken prisoner. Imagine flying for hour after hour in complete darkness over enemy territory, knowing that there was a very high probability that you would be shot down.

Some years ago I was staying with Harold Macmillan at the Mount Nelson in Cape Town and we had dinner on three evenings with Marshal of the Royal Air Force Sir Arthur 'Bomber' Harris. I remember listening to him reminiscing about the war and thinking of those 1,000-bomber raids which he ordered. And I mused on the paradox that in one sense it must have been easier for a young man simply to carry out an order to go on such a mission than for the Commander-in-Chief to shoulder the burden of giving the order, each of them knowing the likely consequences.

My time with PRU was not to last for long, but the time I spent at Benson will always be engraved on my memory. The carefree evenings spent with fellow pilots in the glorious Oxfordshire countryside. In the daytime, the sorties over enemy territory wondering how it was all going to end. The satisfaction in a mission successfully accomplished. The sadness when a colleague did not return. And, through it all, the thrill and joy of flying. There was a young Canadian pilot officer called John Gillespie Magee who was killed in action when he was only nineteen years old. Before he died he wrote this verse:

Oh I have slipped the surly bonds of earth
And danced the skies on laughter-silvered wings;
Sunward I've climbed and joined the tumbling mirth
Of sun-split clouds – and done a hundred things
You have not dreamed of – wheeled and soared and swung
High in the sun-lit silence. Hov'ring there
I've chased the shouting wind along and flung
My eager craft through footless halls of air,
Up, up the long delirious burning blue.
I've topped the wind-swept heights with easy grace
Where never lark nor even eagle, flew;
And while with silent, lifting mind I've trod

The high untrespassed sanctity of space,
Put out my hand and touched the face of God.

On my last flight I was returning from Gibraltar. Very soon after reaching 30,000 feet I was over ten-tenths cloud and it stayed that way without a single break until I had used up more than half the fuel. Eventually came the first welcome break in the cloud but, to my dismay, there was nothing but water as far as the eye could see. I knew that I must be somewhere over the Bay of Biscay, but by this time I should have been hitting the Brest peninsula. What I did not know was that I had been flying into a strong and wholly unexpected head wind which now made it impossible for me to reach England before the fuel ran out. I plodded on and got as far as the Channel coast.

Because it was thought (erroneously as we later found out) that the Germans did not know that our aircraft were unarmed, there was a standing instruction that, in the event of trouble over enemy territory, the aircraft should always be abandoned to destruction. This was doubly important in my case because I was carrying some particularly sensitive photographs of ports in neutral Spain, which were suspected of harbouring German submarines. Fortunately, a second set of photographs was being sent home by more conventional means. The obvious answer was to bale out, and I can still see so vividly that aircraft spiralling to destruction while I floated slowly down to Mont-St-Michel to be greeted by the enemy.

It was an SS unit which was waiting for me as I touched down on the beach – though 'touched down' is not perhaps the best way of describing the sudden impact as I struck the ground. I am sure that at some stage in my training I must have been told how to ease the landing. Alas! I did not remember it then – and I ended up with a badly sprained ankle.

The SS behaved impeccably. After I had released the parachute and disentangled myself, I left it in a heap on the ground. An officer made signs to me to gather it up and, despite the fact that I was limping and obviously in considerable pain, made me carry it as I was marched up the hill to what I suppose was their headquarters.

I do not know how many thousands of pilgrims, over the years, must have made their way up that narrow, steep, winding road to the 900-year-old abbey at the top, to worship there; or how many tens of thousands of tourists in later years have made the same ascent, but I must surely have been the first to have hobbled up with a sprained ankle carrying a parachute in his arms.

The depression of being taken prisoner did not come until later when I found myself alone. At that stage all kinds of thoughts were racing through my mind. I remember thinking of the WAAFs whom I had been taken to see packing with such meticulous care the parachutes on which a life might depend. But my abiding recollection is of the crowds of French men, women and children who had seen me floating down and who were now lining the steep street as I limped along carrying my parachute. These were our allies. Yet not one of them gave even a surreptitious gesture of encouragement. There were no V signs. Maybe they had good reason simply to stare. I suppose I should have remembered those brave men and women in the Resistance but if I am to give an honest account of my feelings at that time I have to admit that I thought to myself: 'Bloody French.'

4
Prisoner of War

From Mont-St-Michel I was taken to a transit camp near Frankfurt, where I was held in solitary and interrogated for a week or so. I had baled out over the sea but, while the aircraft had gone directly down into the sea, that same strong headwind which had prevented me from getting back to base had also blown me back to the shore. Because of this, the Germans apparently never saw the aircraft. Not surprisingly, they were puzzled. What was an Army officer doing arriving by parachute on the Channel coast? What sort of aircraft had dropped me? How many crew were there in the aircraft? To these and other questions I simply played dumb and refused to give any information other than my name, rank and number. Looking back, the interrogation was not unreasonable.

Next came a rather smooth man in civilian clothes who spoke perfect English, said he was from the International Red Cross in Geneva, that he wanted to help me but that he could not inform my next of kin that I was alive unless I was prepared to give more information. Of course, he was bogus. He was nothing to do with the Red Cross. It was a rather naive ruse about which we had been forewarned.

One consequence of my refusal to give more information was that it was some considerable time before it was known that I had been taken prisoner. Because of this, a number of people assumed that I had been killed and I still have a bundle of letters of condolence to my parents – all saying what a good chap I was!

From the transit camp I was moved to Spangenberg, a grim medieval moated castle near Kassel. There were some 200 senior Army officers, the most senior British officer being General Fortune of the 51st Highland Division. Many had been captured at Calais in 1940, and I then realised, for the first time, what being taken prisoner meant to a Regular officer. These men were to lose five years of the most valuable experience a professional soldier could have. In addition, they had no chance of promotion. At least those of us who were amateurs did not have to suffer these disadvantages.

At Spangenberg the British Army officers were well turned out and behaved towards the German officers with impeccable formality. The Germans responded likewise. By contrast the handful of about forty Royal Air Force officers who joined them seemed an unkempt bunch, and it was not surprising that the particular part of the castle which we inhabited became known as the 'Arab Quarter'. Because of my khaki uniform my Air Force colleagues soon christened me 'The Brown Job'. The chances of escaping from the castle were not good but, as it happened, we were soon to be moved on.

It was at Spangenberg that I first met Oliver Philpott, known as 'Ollie', who was later to escape in the 'Wooden Horse' and make his way home via Sweden. He went specially up to Yorkshire to see my parents. They were thrilled to have a first-hand account of the sort of life we were leading.

On leaving Spangenberg we travelled in cattle trucks with one armed guard in each truck. I had acquired a makeshift saw. Ollie organised a posse of men around me while I worked through the night to saw a hole in the floor of the truck. Unhappily, time was not on my side. Before the job was done, the train ground to its final halt. We had arrived at Stalag Luft III, the main camp for Allied air crew. It was purpose-built and set in a large forest clearing just outside the town of Sagan in Silesia.

It was here, in Stalag Luft III, that I made up my mind to put everything into the effort to escape. There were some extraordinary ideas floating around, but there was an efficient escape organisation which had to approve each project. This was essential to avoid one scheme conflicting with another. There was a remarkable forgery department (known as 'Dean and Dawson') producing identity cards, letters of authorisation and travel documents. There were rubber stamps made from the rubber heels taken off shoes. We had a naval officer who in civilian life was a nutrition expert. He would produce concentrated fudge-like bars with a high nutritional value made of sugar, oatmeal, cocoa, etc.

Photographs were essential for identity cards. Sometimes the photograph of a look-alike brother sent from England would be adequate. On one occasion I was involved in a particularly brazen exploit. A young German guard had come into the camp to take photographs of certain prisoners for official identification purposes. He set up his Leica on a tripod and, while his attention was distracted, someone quickly swivelled the camera off the tripod. When the poor guard turned around, his camera was gone. We got the remainder of the thirty-six exposures and, after some quick photography, returned the empty camera. I cannot remember how we managed to get them printed, but we did.

Douglas Bader was always keen to take part in any worthwhile attempt to escape, but his trouble was that his artificial legs made too much noise. A great variety of schemes were considered, some of them non-starters, but some which today seem somewhat outrageous nearly worked. For instance, there was the plan to get into a German airfield, steal an aircraft and fly home. It was not such a far-fetched idea. We had details of the cockpits of several German aircraft and on one occasion, two pilots did actually get into the cockpit of an aircraft. Unfortunately they could not get it started.

We had noticed that a number of laundry bags were collected at regular intervals and taken into a hut in the outer compound of the camp from which it would be relatively easy to get away. They were stored there to await collection. This routine never varied, and so I was packed into one of the bags, duly loaded on to a truck but then – for some unknown reason – all the bags were dumped by the gate of the inner compound. And there I stayed, perspiring profusely. After a while I must have moved slightly, for I heard some shouting and someone kicked the bag. Soon I was surrounded by half a dozen guards with fixed bayonets. I was not allowed to get out of the bag until an officer arrived, during which time I was able, within the bag, to tear my forged documents into minute pieces. Then it was off for a couple of weeks in the cooler.

There were other attempts, but there are two which I think are worth recounting in some detail. They both involved tunnelling, but of a very different kind.

One of the major problems of tunnelling was the dispersal of the earth. Remember that, day and night, the camp was patrolled by specially trained security guards, known as 'ferrets'. So the first difficulty to be overcome was to avoid being seen carrying the earth away from the tunnel, and the second was to put it somewhere where with any luck the ferrets would not find it. Nobody had yet found any way of avoiding these problems. Indeed, they were assumed to be inevitable, for how could you possibly dig a tunnel

without carrying the earth away and dumping it somewhere else?
But it was not inevitable.

I do not know who first thought of the idea but one day while I
was talking and plotting with Tommy Calnan (also a PRU pilot,
who after the war became chief test pilot at Farnborough), he mentioned the concept of 'the mole'. Suppose, instead of digging the
traditional type of tunnel of 100 feet or more, we were to dig a
tunnel only long enough for three men to lie horizontally, one in
front of the other, with a reasonable amount of spare tunnel behind. Suppose then that the earth were to be passed to the back of
the tunnel but, instead of being taken out of the tunnel and secretly
dispersed, were simply used to fill up the spare space in the tunnel
behind us. The theory was strikingly simple and clearly had great
advantages.

All conventional tunnels had a trap at the entrance and, the trap
being inside the camp, this was the part of the tunnel most likely to
be discovered by the Germans, however cleverly camouflaged and
hidden. In the case of the mole there would be no entrance to be
discovered for it would be filled in and no longer exist.

The second advantage was that moling would avoid most of the
delay involved in the secret dispersal of the earth, which was extremely time consuming and frequently had to stop with the approach of one of the ferrets.

The problems were obvious. In the traditional type of tunnel
with a trap at the entrance, it was not too difficult to provide fresh
air for the man at the face. But moving along mole-like in a
completely enclosed underground 'capsule' there would be no fresh
air. We had to find an answer to this. Furthermore, we doubted
whether we could stand the strain of lying prostrate working in
such a confined space for more than twenty-four hours.

This meant that the tunnel had to be reasonably short. And of
course, unlike the traditional tunnel which was shored up with bed
boards, there could be no such support in the mole and we had to
face the very real danger that the earth would give way and collapse
on us.

As luck would have it, sometime later the ideal situation
presented itself to us. The security arrangements round the
perimeter of the compound consisted of two high barbed wire
fences, about six feet apart, filled to the top with coiled barbed
wire. Between this impregnable barrier and the camp proper there

was a strip of ground some twenty feet wide, at the inner border of which was a single strand of trip wire. The whole of this twenty-foot strip was visible to the guards in the high observation towers which were placed round the perimeter barrier. The guards were armed with machine guns and it was well understood that if you stepped over the trip wire into the 'no man's land', you would be shot without warning.

The opportunity to put our theory into practice came when the Germans started to dig a trench in this 'no man's land', the purpose of which was to intercept any shallow tunnels. The trench was sufficiently deep to enable a person to lie in it and – crucial to our plan – to be out of the angle of fire of the guards in their observation towers. We were assured beyond doubt that this blind spot existed. It had been carefully worked out by one of our colleagues, a navigator, who in private life was a chartered surveyor. The problem was how to get over the trip wire and into the trench when the guards in the two nearest observation towers had an unobstructed view of the whole area – apart from the bottom of the trench.

The answer was two completely successful diversions which were set up to attract the attention of the guards. In the first case a group of prisoners rushed to the trip wire to ask the guard in one of the observation towers to telephone for help because of a fire in one of the huts. He obligingly turned his back and went to the telephone. In the other case, two prisoners started a mock fight surrounded by a small crowd near the second observation tower. I was told afterwards that the scene would have done credit to any Western.

The diversions worked perfectly, and before long all three of us had leapt into the trench unseen. We got to work immediately. We tunnelled only a few feet under the surface, where the earth above was firm with the roots of pine trees which had been cut down. Every so often we pushed up a rod to provide an air hole.

As time went on we were faced with two problems, one manageable and one fatal. The first problem was that our third colleague, who shall remain nameless, became claustrophobic. An otherwise tough airman, he began to panic. We had packed a considerable amount of earth behind us and were moving along quite well. He wanted us to go into reverse and to dig our way back to the entrance. There we were in the middle of the night, three sweating individuals lying prostrate in the narrowest of tunnels, blocked at both ends, arguing as to which way we should go!

The truth is that Tommy and I were also pretty whacked. And we were worried because, although the scheme was working, we were not inching forward quite as fast as we had hoped. We knew that we had to get out before dawn, because we were going to surface in a ditch which was only just beyond the far side of the outer wire. We hit the compound side of the wire before first light, but we had still six feet to go to get to the other side of the outer wire, and we knew that there was no chance of making it. Our third man had calmed down and, to his credit, agreed that we should lie in the tunnel throughout the day ready to break out when darkness fell. Whether the three of us could have stuck it for a further twelve hours, we shall never know.

We were resting as best we could, when we heard excited German voices. The alsatians which accompanied the regular perimeter patrol had sniffed at the air-holes and started to bark. Our fear was that the earth might collapse on top of us, so we broke the roof ourselves to see the muzzle of a rifle and looks of absolute astonishment on the face of the guards. It seemed only seconds before the whole camp had assembled to witness the end. They gave us an almighty cheer as we were marched off for yet another period of solitary in the cooler.

5
Escaping

It was shortly afterwards that some of us were sent to Schubin in Poland. The idea of moving us much further east was said to be to make escaping more difficult. In the event, it proved to be easier and thirty of us escaped through what I believe to be the cleverest tunnel of them all.

One of the problems which faced aircrew attempting to escape was that the Germans had decided that, for security reasons, we should never be taken outside the camp to work. On the other hand, we had among us almost every kind of expert and tradesman you could think of, and we received very considerable help, by devious means, from the authorities in London.

So it was that, soon after arriving in Schubin, we set about or-ganising a series of tunnels, most of which were discovered by the Germans at an early stage, but one of which was to prove com-pletely successful.

The Germans knew that the normal trap at the entrance to a tunnel was horizontal. You lifted it up, went down a short shaft and then entered the tunnel itself. One reason why almost all tun-nels were eventually discovered before they made much progress was that, however well the traps were disguised, there was only a limited number of places where they could be located. The huts were pretty spartan, and it was therefore difficult to hide or disguise a trap. The Germans knew all about false floors. On one occasion, after much preparatory work, we moved the whole of an inside wall of a hut some two feet and sunk a shaft in the resulting gap. For a time that looked like being a real winner, but eventually it was discovered, and thereafter the Germans regularly went round meticulously measuring the internal dimensions of each hut in the camp.

It seemed that every conceivable type of trap had been tried, and that the Germans were now familiar with all the old tricks. And yet there was, in theory at least, one concept which had never been pursued because it seemed to be a contradiction in terms. This was the concept of a vertical trap which would be below ground level and out of sight. No one had ever found anywhere where such a trap could be located. But there was such a place at Schubin – in the latrine. It was a remarkable communal seventy-seater and, provided the relevant seats were occupied, no inquisitive German would suspect that work was going on in the enormous pit below. The plan was to made a trap in the side of the pit, below the seats. This would enable us to work in the tunnel undisturbed and, furthermore, we could disperse the earth in the pit itself. The working conditions could hardly be described as ideal, but the whole concept became a brilliant reality.

There was no particular difficulty in making part of the seating detachable, but making the trap in the side of the brick wall of the pit without falling into the pit itself proved to be quite a task. However, it was accomplished. Behind the trap and under the concrete floor we dug out a large chamber six feet high, about twelve feet long and ten feet wide. Nothing on this scale had ever been accomplished before. The great advantage was that the earth from the tunnel could be temporarily stored in the chamber, so enabling digging to continue without the need for immediate dispersal. Some thirty men were involved in the whole operation.

From time to time the Polish workmen were brought into the camp under armed guard to pump out the pit. They soon realised what was happening but typically, despite the risk to themselves, they kept their silence and made our escape possible. We had noted that the pit was never wholly emptied. The level was simply kept down. This meant that the earth from the tunnel would always be covered. We had approximately 130 feet of tunnel to dig to reach a potato clamp which was well outside the perimeter wire, and we aimed to be about twenty feet below ground at the lowest point under the wire.

Fresh air at the tunnel face was essential. Our air-conditioning system was both simple and effective – a kit bag with circles of wire stitched round it so that it acted as a bellows leading into a pipe made of tins laid along the tunnel floor to the man at the face. The operator pumped the kit bag like an upright concertina. The only disadvantage was that the 'fresh air' intake had to be located in the latrine. There was no such thing as a torch, so our light was provided by small tins filled with fat, into each of which was stuck a piece of pyjama cord. Work at the face was hard, and hauling back the earth through more than a hundred feet of a tunnel which was only about two feet high and two feet wide was a considerable task.

While we were making steady progress with the tunnel, all the back-up services were hard at work to prepare for the actual escape. 'Tailors' were transforming uniforms into civilian clothes; the forgery department were turning out identity documents; others were preparing the chunks of concentrated high-energy food.

Once the tunnel had reached beyond the wire, the excitement was intense. The Germans had not the slightest suspicion. Then came the day when we estimated we had reached the point just before the potato clamp and a hollow in the ground next to it. This was to give maximum cover when we broke ground. I shall never forget the moment when I gingerly peeped above the exit hole and waited for the roving searchlight to pass by before wriggling out and along the potato clamp and then away into the woods.

The following morning everyone was apparently assembled as normal for the first count of the day. The report to the Commandant was that thirty prisoners were missing. Twice more the count took place. On each occasion with the same result. The Commandant's reaction was precisely as we had hoped and expected. He simply refused to believe that the missing thirty were not hidden somewhere in the camp. Hour after hour the search proceeded and still the Commandant refused to sound the alarm and report to his superiors that thirty of his prisoners were missing. Meanwhile, those of us who were on the run were given a head start.

My plan was to travel by train from the Polish city of Bromberg back into Germany and up to the Baltic port of Kolberg, where I knew I could get to the Danish island of Bornholm. My Danish relatives on Bornholm would certainly be able to arrange for a herring fishing boat to take me to neutral Sweden. One of my friends in the camp was a Dane and, because of my Danish connections, we discussed travelling together. In the end I decided to go it alone. He, poor man, got as far as Denmark but never made it to Sweden. The rumour was that he drowned.

I spoke some German and any deficiency in my accent was accounted for by my posing as a Danish *freiwilliger* – a Danish volunteer workman. I had a forged foreign worker's identity card and I was dressed in trousers dyed brown, wearing a RAF raincoat, which to the Germans bore no resemblance to a military coat, and a cap which a helpful Pole had conveniently left behind on one of the visits to clear out the latrine. I had a small attaché case containing some concentrated food, shaving kit, a cloth to keep my shoes clean and so on. Most of my fellow escapees would be walking by night and hiding by day. For them appearance was secondary. For me, travelling by train, it was essential not to appear dishevelled.

I had sixteen miles to walk to the railway station at Bromberg and I had to be there to catch the morning train. I walked mainly on the railway track itself, but skirted stations and signal boxes which was very time-consuming. Walking along the track was awkward because the sleepers were just too close together for a normal stride. Anyway I got to the outskirts of Bromberg and cleaned myself up before walking into the town.

My plan was to leave the train at Schneidemuhl and then to travel north to Kolberg. I had plenty of German money, cleverly smuggled into the camp from London, and I was therefore able to ask for a return ticket, as a means of avoiding suspicion. It was with some trepidation that I went up to the ticket office and said 'Schneidemuhl, hin und zuruck, bitte.' No problem. So I checked the platform and when I got there who should I see walking up and down but Tommy Calnan and Robert Kee who were travelling together. Tommy, in his book *Free as a Running Fox*, recalls the encounter thus:

> I was watching a very smart young man as he walked up and down the platform. He was wearing a neat blue-grey rain-coat, carrying an attaché case and had a folded newspaper tucked under his arm. He looked like a superior bank clerk. There was something vaguely familiar about him, but I did not recognise him until he passed close to us.
>
> It was Tony Barber.
>
> Tony recognised me at the same time and very deliberately looked the other way. But I could not resist getting up to greet him. His look of panic when he saw me coming should have discouraged me, but I was enjoying the moment too much. I gave him a nicely casual Nazi salute and greeted him.
>
> 'Heil Hitler,' I said.
>
> He was forced to respond in the same way and to return my salute.

I then shook hands with him and told him how delighted I was to see him.

'Go to hell,' said Tony. He was shaking with anger. 'And stay away from me. You look like a tramp.' With great self-control, he shook hands again and bowed himself away. When the train came in he made a point of boarding it a considerable distance from us.

There were three classes of travel on the train. Although I had plenty of money and was reasonably well dressed, I was not quite smart enough to appear as an obvious first-class passenger. Because the Germans would naturally assume that any escaped prisoner travelling by train would be short of cash, they would expect him to travel third class. So I travelled second class.

I entered the compartment, took my seat as casually as I could and raised my eyes to glance around. For a moment I froze. There sitting opposite me and looking out of the window was a German NCO whom I immediately recognised as coming from the camp. I dared not change compartments for fear of exciting suspicion, so I stayed put. The man never recognised me and in fact, although I did not know it at the time no alarm had yet been given by the camp Commandant.

When we got to Schneidemuhl, I joined Tommy and Robert and we walked together out of the town. In Tommy's words:

Tony had completely recovered his good temper. There was nobody about and we talked freely and happily, relating our experiences of the night before. We were all in high spirits. Soon Tony left us to return to the station. He was taking a different route, aiming at the Baltic coast. He had some rather mysterious plan for getting to the island of Bornholm. We wished him luck, sorry to see him go.

I found that there was no train going north until the following morning, so I walked out of the town again and into the woods where I eventually settled down for the night. I had nothing to keep me warm and by midnight it had started to drizzle and I was shivering in the damp cold of an East European March night. With the temperature falling, it was impossible to spend the night in the open and, in any event, I had to keep up a reasonably clean appearance. I could see no buildings in the countryside. To wander round in the middle of the night looking for shelter in some outhouse on the outskirts of the town would inevitably have appeared furtive to anyone who spotted me.

So often on such occasions the least risky course is the brazen one. I walked back into the empty town and, with all the false confidence I could muster, I entered the railway station and made for the waiting room. It was packed with German soldiers drinking beer from the buffet. There were virtually no civilians. I went up to the counter. 'Ein bier, bitte.' This, together with a bowl of potato soup, made me one of the crowd and, with a limited amount of conversation, a few more beers and the occasional doze, the night passed uneventfully.

It was on the next leg of my journey that some plain clothes police came through the train checking the papers of each passenger. I sensed that this was no routine check, and my suspicion was confirmed when I overheard a reference to escaped prisoners of war. But all went well. My identity papers were accepted without demur, as was my story that I was travelling to see my brother, also a Dane, who was ill.

My confidence was growing, I was getting used to being in the company of Germans, the sense of being hunted was receding and more than ever before I really began to believe that I was going to make it. I had now reached a small town in northern Pomerania, and had only one more comparatively short train journey to complete before reaching Kolberg. There were a couple of hours to wait for the train, it was a crisp sunny Sunday morning, and I set off to walk round the town, not strolling, but always with a purposeful air. There were plenty of people about, I was many miles from the camp and there was nothing to arouse suspicion.

I saw two elderly SA men, 'Brownshirts', walking slowly along the footpath towards me. Quite casually, it seemed almost on the spur of the moment, they stopped as we were passing each other and asked for my papers. They were not in the least aggressive, but they exuded the dogged perseverance of the minor official. They returned my identity papers and accepted my story but they pointed out that, as a foreign volunteer worker, I should have a letter from my German employer giving me permission to be away from my place of work. I knew before the escape that this was the one piece of paper I was lacking, but the camp's forgery department had simply not had time to prepare it.

'You say you are here to visit your sick brother. Where is he living?' one of them asked. I had noticed we were in a street called Friedrichstrasse. 'Friedrichstrasse siebzehn,' I replied, hoping they would leave me to go on my way. Not so. They may not have looked particularly bright, but they were stubborn. They said they would come with me. We arrived at the door of no. 17 and I rang the bell. A lady answered the door.

I explained that I had come to visit my brother who was ill. She replied that the only people who lived in the house were her own family. I knew in my heart that the end was not far away, but I thought that there might be just a chance that, although the SA men were armed, an opportunity would arise to make a dash for it. So it seemed worthwhile to play them along for a little longer. We walked together to the police station where they said they would telephone my employer. Once we had entered the building, all chance of escape had gone, and the game was up. 'Ich bin ein Offizier in der Britischer Luftwaffe.'

Depressed as I was, I shall never forget the astonishment on their faces. Instead of checking out some poor little Danish workman who was taking a couple of days off without permission, they had made a great catch. Within the hour I was bundled into a car and taken to the Gestapo headquarters back in Schneidemuhl.

For a week I was kept there, interrogated for long periods during the night and made to stand up in my cell for several hours during the day. I was never physically ill-treated, but on several occasions I heard the cries of others who were. I was repeatedly reminded during the interrogations that none of my colleagues knew where I was or what had happened to me and that I was entirely at the mercy of the Gestapo. They could do with me whatever they wished and nobody would ever know. Who had given me the money? Where had I got the cap from? What were the plans of the others who had got out of the tunnel?

My mind went back to a discussion some of us had had soon after being taken prisoner. We had concluded that once you told your inquisitors anything, even if false, they would know that you were on the slide. And in those circumstances the Gestapo would not hesitate to use physical force and, if you were left a wreck, to dispose of you.

One day, during the afternoon, I was collected from my cell, and taken upstairs to what turned out to be my final interrogation. My reaction to the questions was the same as on all the previous occasions. This time there were two interrogators and one of them pointed out yet again that, as far as my comrades were concerned, I had simply disappeared, that I was entirely in the hands of the Gestapo and that, unless I co-operated, I would be taken out and shot there and then. I referred lamely to the Geneva Convention, and they smiled. There was a short silence, and I was taken roughly by the arms, out of the room, down the stairs and into a yard. I was then told that I had one last chance to co-operate. I cannot now recall what I felt, except that I accepted that the end had come and I longed for just one friend. I said nothing.

To me it was desperately real. I did not know that to the man who had interrogated me for a week it was a ruse – one last attempt to get me to talk. Then: 'Take him back to his cell.'

Within what I seem to remember was an hour or so I was taken to the same railway station which I had last seen a week previously. I was then escorted under armed guard back to the camp in Poland. Just before I left my cell I had torn off the bottom of the prison instructions which were hanging on the wall. On that bit of paper was a large and very clear rubber stamp with the swastika in the middle and around the edge the dreaded words 'Geheime Staatspolizei' – Secret State Police, or Gestapo. I hid the bit of paper in my shoe and I knew that our forgery boys back in the camp would be thrilled.

Eventually, after a period of solitary, I learned that all thirty of us had been caught and brought back to the camp, except for the Dane and his companion who were missing. Our only satisfaction, apart from the excitement and a short spell of freedom, was that we had caused untold havoc to the German authorities. There was nothing else to do except to settle down to plan the next escape.

When I came out of the cooler I was told that, despite the most intensive search, the Germans had failed to find the entrance to the tunnel. They were furious. Then they found the exit by the potato clamp. So they brought along a terrified Russian prisoner, tied a rope to his leg and ordered him to crawl back through the tunnel. The poor man must have got quite a surprise when he ended up in a latrine!

6
Uneasy Liberation

Shortly after the escape from Schubin, we were sent back to the East Compound of Stalag Luft III at Sagan. Then, early in April 1944, something happened which altered my whole attitude to escaping. Seventy-six prisoners had escaped through a tunnel from the North Compound. When it was discovered, a team of Gestapo and SS men arrived in the compound and, after investigations, the German Commandant was removed and many of the German staff were court-martialled. Then came the awful news. The new Commandant summoned the Senior British Officer in each compound and told them that he had been instructed to make the following report: 'The Senior British Officer is to be informed that as a result of a tunnel from which seventy-six officers escaped from Stalag Luft III, North Compound, forty-one of these officers have been shot whilst resisting arrest or attempting further escape after arrest.'

The Commandant said that he was not authorised to answer questions but, when pressed, he did say that he thought that no one had been wounded. It was, of course, inconceivable that, if his account had been genuine, some of the forty-one prisoners would not have been wounded. In fact, it turned out that not forty-one but fifty of our colleagues had been shot and, towards the end of April, fifty cremation urns were brought to the compound, each of which bore the name of one of the prisoners who had been murdered.

There were other depressing periods. When things were going particularly badly for the Allies, we were informed that Hitler had decreed that after the war all RAF aircrew would spend twelve years helping to rebuild German cities. Then there was the occasion when one of our colleagues went berserk and tried to scale the wire in broad daylight. It was obvious that he could not have escaped, yet the guards shot him dead. There were those sad personal cases, too, where a prisoner received news of some family tragedy which was particularly hard to bear in a situation where it was physically impossible to comfort those at home. Perhaps more hurtful for a prisoner was the rare case when, month after month when mail arrived for the rest of us, there would be none for him. Living in such close confinement where there was absolutely no privacy – even the latrines were communal – you could soon sense when a colleague was in low spirits.

Yet, by and large, our morale remained high. After all, we did not begin to suffer anything approaching the terrible privations of those who were captured by the Japanese. We were all young and, because we had been selected for aircrew, we were pretty fit. And we had our fun.

There was the new pompous German Commandant who told the Senior British Officer that we were to salute him whenever we passed him in the compound. When it was explained that RAF officers did not salute without hats, he said we should greet him. It was not long before someone realised that he spoke no English and so, with a respectful smile, greeted him with the words: 'Good morning, you f . . . . old b . . . . . . ' The Commandant replied, with an equally affable smile: 'Guten morgen, meine herren.'

Then there was the wine which we made for Christmas. We saved up raisins and sugar from Red Cross parcels and managed to get some yeast. The wine was absolutely revolting, so there was only one thing to do. We concocted a still which we kept in one of the tunnels. The resulting spirit was rather like an inferior bicycle oil and was quite lethal.

One aspect of POW life, which is perhaps not surprising, was the fact that rank became far less important than personality. I mention just one example. When I arrived at Stalag Luft III there was one man in particular who seemed to be involved with almost everything that was going on; and that was Aidan Crawley. At the beginning of the war he had been with the Balkan Intelligence Service – Turkey, Bulgaria and Yugoslavia. Smuggled out via Belgrade, he returned to flying and was captured after being shot down in North Africa. Now he was a member of the Escape Committee, responsible for collecting information and intelligence which might be useful for escapers. He was a fluent German speaker and was with us on the escape from Poland. He got almost as far as the Swiss frontier before being caught.

When he was not involved in activities associated with escaping, Aidan was organising other events. He was even responsible for the choreography for a Christmas show in which I was given the part of a black lady dancing to some Negro spiritual! A staunch supporter of the Labour Party, he arranged a series of political debates which gave him the opportunity to put the case for Labour. In 1945 he became the Labour Member of Parliament for Buckingham. In 1957 he resigned from the Labour Party and in 1962 became the Conservative Member of Parliament for West Derbyshire. But many Labour members never forgave him for leaving them, and many Conservative members never really accepted him.

After the murder of those fifty colleagues, I began to have serious doubts about the wisdom of continuing to attempt to escape. I think that I have always been fairly realistic and I came to the conclusion that for a number of reasons further attempts to get out of Stalag Luft III were simply not worth the candle. The guards had been doubled, some form of listening device had been installed to detect tunnelling, and the reality was that in the new situation even if one got out of the compound, the chances of getting home were not such as to make worthwhile the very real possibility of being shot. Besides, I was confident we were winning the war.

I therefore decided to banish thoughts of escaping from my mind and to concentrate entirely on working for the final of my law degree. The Red Cross supplied the camps with large numbers of books, which the German authorities welcomed, assuming that this would keep the prisoners out of mischief. Very early on after being captured, I had asked for the necessary law books. It was a long shot, but eventually they did arrive and so for the next few months I spent almost every working hour absorbed in the law.

I was now twenty-four. The thought of having my law degree behind me when I arrived home was the real spur to what was really an exercise in cramming. It was not as difficult as it might seem because, after all, there were no serious distractions. The International Red Cross arranged for the examination papers to be sent out and late in 1944 I sat the examination under the watchful eye of a wing commander who acted as invigilator. Within weeks of completing the exam we were on the move and I was very doubtful as to whether the papers would ever get to England. It was not until I returned home after the war that I was told that, thanks to the International Red Cross, the papers had been delivered to the university authorities and that I had been awarded a degree with first class honours.

On 27 January 1945, with only a few hours' notice, we were told to be ready to march. The Russian advance was getting closer – I heard afterwards that the Russian Army overran the compound ten days later. Because the roads were covered with snow, we set about constructing makeshift sledges out of whatever wood we could find or break off from the huts. Eventually there were 10,000 of us on the move. Every now and then the column would bunch up and those at the rear would stop. There were frequent heavy snow showers, a biting wind and it was bitterly cold. The snow froze on our clothes. The roads were cluttered with German refugees fleeing to the West in terror of the oncoming Russian invaders. They made a pitiful sight and were completely demoralised. We, on the other hand, although suffering the privations of the weather, were in fine spirits, knowing we were on the winning side.

As the days passed, the situation became more and more chaotic – German soldiers, British prisoners, terrified civilians, all intermingled and all concerned for their own survival. Some men collapsed from exhaustion and cold. If they could not continue further they were left behind in German houses. Many of the guards had served on the Russian Front and were not as physically fit as the prisoners. They, too. began to fall by the wayside and were taken in by German families. It would have been all to easy to escape, but the order was given by the Senior British Officer that we were to stay together.

No prior arrangements had been made for billeting at night and yet with temperatures well below freezing it was simply not possible to spend the nights in the open. Fortunately we always managed to find somewhere. I remember arriving at one town at the end of a day's march and having to wait for four hours in the street in the bitter weather before being shepherded into a school. On that occasion many of us suffered quite severe physical pain from standing around in such conditions.

There were two nights which those of us from the East Compound will always remember. One was in a church where we were crammed into every corner – there was even one man sleeping on the altar table. The other night was spent in a glass factory at a place called Muskau. The furnaces were still hot and for the first time for days we were warm and able to dry our clothes. That night is also memorable because of the way in which the management of the factory went out of their way to help, including providing hot drinks. I remember wondering whether it was their humanitarian instincts coming to the fore or whether it was something to do with the advancing Russians being only a few miles away.

Eventually it thawed and the snow began to turn to slush. With the sledges now useless what we needed was something with wheels for we had no back packs. Then came a little bit of luck. I noticed a German woman pushing a pram – happily with no baby in it – and on behalf of a group of us persuaded her to hand over the pram in exchange for some of our food. She was happy enough with her side of the bargain and we had transport for our belongings.

It was now clear to all of us that if we simply continued our slow march west, we would soon be overtaken by the Russian Army. The Germans, however, decided to split us up. The group I was with were locked into the cattle trucks and finally decanted at Luckenwalde, a town south west of Berlin. The camp at Luckenwalde contained some 16,000 prisoners of almost every nationality on the Allied side. The conditions were atrocious. There was very little food and many of the Russian prisoners who had been there for several months were dying of starvation. In addition to the Russians, there were French, Italian, Yugoslavs, Czechs and Norwegians.

We were over 200 in our hut in three-tier bunks. There were no toilet facilities inside the hut and one of my abiding memories is of a never-ending succession, throughout the night, of men climbing down from creaky wooden bunks and shuffling out to make themselves more comfortable. The cold did not help.

The weeks passed and then one day we heard the sound of gunfire. The German guards melted away and, on a Sunday towards the end of April, a Russian armoured car entered the camp. There followed more and more Russians and we knew then, or thought we knew, that at long last we were free. But the Russians would not let us go. Week after week went by. At one stage a convoy of American trucks arrived to collect us. We defied the Russian order to stay in the camp and got on the trucks. The Russians fired over our heads and, not surprisingly, we returned to the camp and the American trucks went back empty. Meanwhile, German women and children were entering the camp and pleading for protection from the Russians.

As the weeks passed, we became increasingly concerned. The Russians continued to refuse to release us. Then we heard that the

British were holding some hundreds of Russian officers and our spirits sank. Were we being held as hostages? VE Day passed and we listened with envy to the celebrations on the radio. Still the Russians would not let us go. Then, at long last, we were free. The Germans used to greet their captives with the words, all too familiar to British POWs, 'Fur sie ist der krieg vorbei', 'For you the war is over'. It was a phrase which now had a happier ring.

Almost half a century later I became chairman of the RAF Benevolent Fund. I accepted the position not only because I looked forward to a continuing association with the RAF, but also because, as I came through the war unscathed, it was not asking much to do something for those who were not so fortunate. Some twelve years ago I had written a chapter for a book entitled *The RAF at War*, published in aid of the Fund. Part of that chapter is reproduced here.

Before agreeing to become involved with any charity there are three questions to be asked. Is it a worthwhile cause? Is it efficiently and economically administered? Shall I enjoy it? In the case of the RAF Benevolent Fund it did not take me long to satisfy myself on all three counts. That a charity should be properly administered is obvious. The trouble is that if the charity is of any size, it is quite impossible for the chairman to know all that is going on. He therefore has to rely on the calibre and character of the staff. The RAF Benevolent Fund is run by retired RAF personnel and is highly efficient. It needs to be, for the Fund spends some £10 million a year on welfare and the relief of distress, and has helped more than 15,000 members of the Air Force Family in each of the least few years. But it would be wrong to think of RAF personnel and their families as being only on the receiving end. It is to me a remarkable and encouraging fact that over 80% of serving members of the RAF voluntarily give to the Fund half a day's pay each year.

One particular aspect of the administration is worth mentioning. Although the staff have authority to make grants within certain limits, most of the grants and loans are sanctioned by one of a number of committees of voluntary workers which meet regularly. The variety of ways in which help is provided is infinite. More often than not the help needed is quite modest but can make all the difference, such as the case of the wife who suffered from arthritis in her hands and whose retired Air Force husband was incontinent. All she wanted was a washing machine.

When I was first approached to become chairman, there was one thing which troubled me, and that was that the Fund's headquarters were located in a magnificent house in Portland Place, which has been described as 'the grandest street in eighteenth-century London'. Should we not have our headquarters in the East End? The answer was that we hold a 973-year lease at a fixed rental of £500 per annum, reduced to £200 per annum so long as the buildings are occupied by the Benevolent Fund. Not a bad deal.

7
Oxford

When I was stationed at Benson we made frequent visits to Oxford, but the idea that after the war I might enter one of the colleges would have seemed far-fetched. It was when I was a prisoner of war, and the course of the war was turning in the Allies' favour, that I began to raise my sights. I decided that, if all went well, I would go to the Bar. And I began to think that maybe it was not so far-fetched to think of going up to Oxford.

As soon as I was demobilised, I pursued the idea. It seemed to me that I had every reason to expect that I would qualify for an ex-serviceman's grant since I appeared to fulfil all the conditions. I was turned down, however, on the grounds that I already had a degree. This seemed to me to be grossly unfair. I was being penalised for having had the initiative and perseverance to work for a degree while a POW. Had I spent the days lying on my back reading thrillers, I might have been awarded a grant. I had almost given up hope when the father of an erstwhile girlfriend of mine was able to put me in contact with Sir Norman Birkett, probably the greatest advocate of his day. He immediately took the point that after more than three years as a POW I needed a period of rehabilitation before starting to practise at the Bar.

'Who is dealing with the application at the Department of Education?' he asked. 'A Miss Lerpinière,' I replied. 'Then we must write to her.' He moved over to a small portable typewriter, typed the letter himself, and soon after I was on my way back to London with the letter in my pocket. It did the trick. Forty years later at a reception at the Westminster Medical School of which I was then Chairman, an elderly lady came up to me and said, 'Do you remember me? My name is Lerpinière. I have often wondered how different your life might have been if I had not changed my mind and awarded you a grant.'

I was accepted by Oriel College which later did me the honour of making me an Honorary Fellow. I had two years of the most enjoyable rehabilitation anyone could wish for. It was like a dream come true.

Because I already had a law degree I decided to broaden my horizon and read politics, philosophy and economics. Also, because I had got a first in law, I have to admit that I decided quite deliberately that there was no particular advantage in getting an outstanding degree and that at the age of twenty-five I would spend the next two years accordingly. I spoke once in a Union debate but thought the whole business rather childish and never attended again. I realise now that had I been younger I would have taken a very different view.

I spent the first year living in college and the second year sharing rooms at No. 1 Holywell with Donald Edgar who was later to become the best William Hickey columnist of them all. Beaverbrook called him a journalist of genius. Donald was much more of an intellectual than I was. He had a greater knowledge of the arts and of music, but we had one thing in common. We had both been POWs and we were both determined to make up for lost time. They were good days. Listening to Mendelssohn's Italian Symphony with a bottle of good claret bought at cost from the manciple in the college, earnest discussions about philosophy with no thought of the fact that soon there would be the need to earn a living, and attending only those lectures which appealed.

Many years later I received a letter urging me to allow my name to go forward for the position of Provost of Oriel. I was assured that there was support. Tempting? Certainly, for I owed much to Oriel. But with the passage of time it was not really for me.

When I came down from Oxford, I still had to pass my Bar Finals. My brother Noel was at that time editor of the *Continental Daily Mail* in Paris, and on one of his visits to London he suggested that I might like to stay with him in Paris and work for my Bar Finals there. This seemed an admirable idea, so I packed a suitcase full of law books and set off for Paris. Noel had a large and luxurious apartment on the Left Bank and I installed myself there with Snell's Equity, Salmon on Tort, Anson on Contract and all the rest to prepare for the last examinations I hoped I would ever have to take. Because of the war years, I was now twenty-seven and I found the whole exam business thoroughly depressing. There was another factor which hung over me and that was that I had been granted an Inner Temple scholarship which was conditional on my passing my Bar Finals first time.

I expect it was illusory, but to me Paris was a city of splendour after the somewhat dreary post-war London. I had very little money but that did not matter. Noel took me everywhere. The mid-morning visits to the Ritz where we each had one of those small bottles of champagne, lunch at the Officers' Club and dinner at Maxim's where they did not seem to have heard of rationing. For some reason I never found out, the wine waiter at Maxim's insisted on calling me 'Mon prince'. Then there was 'Le Sphinx', not to mention other attractions: this was high life indeed. It went on for a fortnight. In the evenings I had not a care in the world, but every morning there loomed the spectre of those dreaded Bar Finals and that conditional Inner Temple scholarship. There was only one thing to do. After two weeks of carefree abandonment I packed up my books and returned to Oxford where my old college generously provided me with a room. There, without distractions, I settled down to serious work.

Then came the week of the Bar Finals, on the outcome of which so much depended. I have always taken the view that if you want something badly enough you should risk everything to get it. And so, although I could not really afford it, I took a room at the Savoy for the period of the examinations and I spent my whole time, other than in the examination room, living on sandwiches and coffee and cramming in my bedroom at the Savoy. It was money well spent. Soon after, I was called to the Bar and made my first appearance at Durham Assizes. My client was an old lag with an appalling record and I persuaded him to plead guilty. I got three guineas. He got seven years. I was on my way.

8
MP for Doncaster

In 1949 the Doncaster Conservative Association was trying to find a candidate to fight what appeared to be a hopeless seat with a Labour majority of more than 23,000. Against the advice of my father, who thought that I should first establish myself at the Bar, and against the advice of the Conservative Central Office, who sent an official to the constituency to tell them that I was not up to the task, I was selected. 'Selected' is perhaps not quite the right word for I was the only applicant. That was really not surprising, bearing in mind the Labour majority, and the fact that there had been only one previous Conservative member for the constituency this century (in the landslide election of 1929). I had done a little speaking for the Conservative Party, including four days at the Hull fish docks which I would not count as a roaring success. To fight an impossible seat would be a useful experience and would stand me in good stead if ever I wanted to apply for a safe seat.

Then came the prerequisite of all success in politics – a little bit of luck. Unbeknown to me, the Parliamentary Boundary Commission was about to alter the constituency boundaries by cutting off two predominantly Labour villages. The General Election came in February 1950 and although a Labour Government was returned, it was left without an adequate working majority. In Doncaster the Labour majority was slashed from more than 23,000 to 878. I knew then that to win was a real possibility and it was obvious that another General Election must come soon. The morale of the local party workers was transformed. In effect all we had to do was to persuade 450 electors to change their political allegiance and we would be home and dry.

That year, 1950, was memorable for another quite different reason. Doncaster was surrounded by safe Labour seats and the most impregnable of them all was the coal-mining constituency of Hemsworth which had the largest Labour majority in the country.

The Conservative candidate was the girl I was to marry in the autumn of that year. She was thirty-year-old Jean Asquith, an Oxford graduate who towards the end of the war had been commissioned in the ATS. We were happily married for thirty-three years, during which she supported me in good times and bad.

During my political career I saw far too little of our children and have always regretted that I was not around to enjoy their formative years as much as I would have had I been in some less disruptive occupation. Jean often had to cope alone with many problems which would normally be shared. But I knew that I could rely on her. She also understood the pressures of political life, having herself fought a General Election. Predictably, she did not win Hemsworth, but her triumph was that she saved her deposit. One other point needs to be made. When I got into the House we both agreed that one politician in the family was quite enough. Sadly, in 1983 she died. By then my political career was over.

The prospect of winning Doncaster for the Conservatives for only the second time this century was a tremendous challenge. I should mention here that the boundaries of the parliamentary constituency of Doncaster were coterminous with the borough boundaries, so the constituency was very compact. This made it ideal for short unannounced open-air 'meetings'. I was said to have the loudest loudspeaker van in Yorkshire!

I would turn up at a corner at the end of a row of terraced houses and play the theme music from a popular radio programme of the time called 'Down Your Way'. The housewives would come out onto the doorstep to see what was happening and then I would start. Very occasionally I would have to move on because somebody's husband was a miner or railway worker who was on nightshift and trying to get some sleep. After ten minutes on the loudspeaker, I would walk up the street to meet anyone who wanted to talk to me.

Members of Parliament have a fund of stories about canvassing, but none quite so embarrassing as the occasion when Dorothy Macmillan said to the lady who answered the door: 'I hope we can rely on you and your husband for your support.' 'I'm afraid my husband died last year,' the lady replied, and added 'but don't worry, I've sent in his postal vote.'

So much for the effort to get the message across. Equally important was organisation. We set about building up a superb organisation with over 500 'block wardens' and we concentrated on postal votes. By the time the next election came, in October 1951, we had organised over 1,500 postal votes, whereas the local Labour Party had got less than 500. We won by a majority of 384. The fact that without that superior organisation we would have lost was a lesson that remained with me when, many years later, I became Chairman of the Party.

So there I was, married, a Member of Parliament with £1,000 a year, out of which I had to pay all my parliamentary expenses including, in particular, the salary of a private secretary.

I had never listened to a debate in the House of Commons (this was long before there was television coverage), indeed I had never been inside the place. So imagine my surprise when the Government Chief Whip, Patrick Buchan-Hepburn, telephoned me to say that Mr Churchill would like me to second the Loyal Address in reply to the King's Speech on the first working day of the new Parliament. That was 6 November 1951.

On my way to London I found myself sitting in the same compartment as Tom Williams, a highly respected and worldly-wise older Labour member who had been in Attlee's Cabinet. He lived in Doncaster and had read that I was to second the Loyal Address. He asked me whether I had prepared my speech. I must have exhibited a certain lack of modesty when I replied that I had, for he then said in his broad Yorkshire accent: 'If I may give you a bit of advice, Tony, I wouldn't appear to be too confident. They don't like it.' It was very sound advice. The one thing the Commons does not like is a cocky new boy.

I had heard that the occasion was somewhat formal and that the mover and seconder of the Address might have to wear morning coats, in which case I would have to take mine down to London. I telephoned the Chief Whip from Yorkshire to seek his advice. He replied that the Prime Minister had decided that we should wear normal dark suits. So down I travelled to London in a dark suit, leaving my morning coat behind.

Then came the eve of the new Parliamentary Session when it is traditional for the Prime Minister to invite the members of his Government to Downing Street to hear the King's Speech. What I did not know was that, in addition to the members of the Government, the mover and seconder of the Address are also invited. So there I was in No. 10. No sooner had I entered the drawing room than the Chief Whip came up to me and said that the Prime Minister would like to see me to congratulate me on winning Doncaster. I had never met Mr Churchill before. He was sitting in the corner of the far drawing room, cigar in hand. I was duly introduced and Mr Churchill, after a few pleasantries about the campaign in Doncaster, made only one further remark: 'You'll be wearing a tail coat tomorrow.' As soon as I left No. 10, I was on the telephone to my home in Yorkshire and the following morning down to London by train came my morning coat.

This was Churchill's one and only peacetime Government and we were in with a majority of only seventeen. But for a handful of other wins like Doncaster the post-war Labour Government would have continued in office for another Parliament. As the new House of Commons assembled to hear the King's Speech, there was an atmosphere of intense excitement and, as I took my place on the second bench, I realised how privileged I was to be taking part in the historic formalities of a new Parliament. It was apparently the first time the Loyal Address had been moved or seconded by a newly elected member. The House was packed and the hubbub grew as we waited expectantly for Black Rod to summon the Commons to the Lords to hear the King's Speech. Then, on our return, the Speaker repeated the Speech and after the mover of the Address had made his speech, it was my turn.

Doncaster, in those days, was renowned not only for horse-racing but also as an important railway centre. I therefore started in what I hoped was a humorous vein, referring to the fact that the trains were more predictable than the horses. (Constituency loyalty prevented my adding that Doncaster was also noted for slow trains and fast women.) It is customary for the seconder of the Address to concentrate on foreign affairs and I pursued the theme that there were three pillars on which we should build for a lasting peace. 'In the first place, we must pursue a foreign policy which is not only consistent but which is clearly known throughout the world. . . . The second pillar on which we must build our plan for peace is to negotiate from strength and not from weakness. . . . The third pillar is to work in the very closest cooperation with our allies.'

Looking back all those years ago, I am slightly unnerved at the self-confidence of the young man, just elected, pontificating on the fundamentals of foreign policy in the presence of Churchill and Eden *et al*. Then followed the customary congratulations from Mr

Attlee, Leader of the Opposition, and the new Prime Minister who referred to my having 'overcome the double ordeal of making a maiden speech in conditions of exceptional formality and importance.'

In due course I retired to the Smoking Room and, after a few whiskies, I found myself thinking that this was the life for me!

9

A Professional Dilemma

If events had not conspired to tempt me into a political career, I should have been equally happy staying at the Bar. I enjoyed tremendously my few years in practice.

A good set of chambers is a sort of fraternity. After the communal life in the Forces and in various prison camps it might be thought that I longed for privacy. Paradoxically, for quite some time after I returned home I found being alone intensely depressing. No doubt the condition would today be graced with a name of a 'syndrome' but, looking back, I think it was a perfectly natural reaction to the quite sudden and intoxicating switch from incarceration to freedom.

Whatever the reason I liked the camaraderie of life in chambers. In the early days I wondered whether, with no contacts of my own, I would get enough work to keep me going. And so, with time on my hands, when I was not listening to cases in court, I would repair with other under-employed barristers to the Kardomah coffee shop in Fleet Street.

Happily, it was not long before I was getting enough work to pay my way. Instead of morning coffee at the Kardomah, now it was drinks after court at El Vino's. I was beginning to feel part of the establishment. Whether I was with fellow juniors or talking with some eminent Silk I was equally at home. Determined to look the instant veteran, instead of buying a new wig – all white and looking like nylon (which it probably was) – I acquired an old secondhand grey horsehair wig from some retired 'Rumpole' at the Old Bailey.

During those early years at the Bar I was more than content with my lot. When I was asked to stand for Doncaster I was just beginning to make my way and, on any rational assessment, I should have concentrated on the law. Although I was in London chambers, most of my work initially was on the North Eastern Circuit. The

Leader of the Circuit was an outstanding advocate called Harry Hylton-Foster who was also the Conservative Member of Parliament for York (and later Speaker of the House of Commons). He seemed the obvious man from whom to seek advice, so I telephoned his clerk and arranged to meet him for tea at the Station Hotel at York. I explained my problem and sought his advice as to whether, at such an early stage in my career at the Bar, I could combine it with the House of Commons. He replied with a smile: 'I don't think you really want my advice. What you really want is for me to agree with you that you should go ahead. If that's how you feel, I should do just that.'

There were four assize cities on the North Eastern Circuit – York, Leeds, Newcastle and Durham. For the newcomer in a set of chambers it was the clerk who initially held your future in his hands. If he liked you, he could ensure that you got the work; but whether you made the most of the opportunity and performed well was up to you. Soon I was not only getting the work but also enjoying the social life as we travelled round the Circuit. In those days there was a Bar mess in each of the four assize cities and, in at least two of them, we had our own wine cellar.

Before long, I was elected 'Junior of the Circuit' which was somewhat of a misnomer for it did not mean that you were the most junior barrister. It was an honorary position, carrying with it certain obligations and certain benefits. I mention only one obligation and one benefit, the combination of which proved to be a stern test of character. The obligation was always to be the last person to leave the table after dinner and the benefit was the right to unlimited free port throughout the evening.

So there I would find myself late in the evening, sitting alone with some fashionable Silk who had come down from London for an exorbitant fee, won his case, and was biding his time at the dinner table until the moment came to board the night sleeper back to London. As the port came round yet again, I had to exercise considerable self-restraint to ensure that I would be up to the mark for my own modest cause célèbre the following morning.

As my work at the Bar grew, I was finding it more and more difficult to combine it with the House of Commons. It was not so much the volume of work, for I could always work at weekends and on weekdays in the Commons Library. The problem was quite simply that I could not be in two places at once – in court on circuit and in the Commons at Westminster. The answer was to move to some branch of the law which involved less court work.

And so I moved from 5 Paper Buildings to 6 King's Bench Walk to join a set of chambers specialising entirely in taxation. I missed the life on circuit and I missed the excitement of court work, but at least it was now possible to combine my career at the Bar with the House of Commons. I certainly could not count on the latter to keep the home fires burning. My pay as a Member of Parliament was still only £1,000 a year. But my concern was not only with the short term. What did the future hold for a member with a majority of less than 400 out of a total electorate of some 60,000?

Then there was another development. It was being put about in my constituency that I was looking for a safer seat and that, if I were offered one, I would abandon Doncaster. I was very conscious of the fact that I owed my good fortune to all those loyal Conservative workers who had sent me to Westminster. What would they think if, like some old-time carpetbagger, I were to abandon them for lusher pastures? There was only one thing to do. I issued a public statement in which I committed myself to continue to stand for the Doncaster constituency unless and until I lost it.

Work at the Tax Bar was exacting, but financially very rewarding, and partly no doubt because I was fortunate to be in the leading Tax chambers, I soon built up a lucrative practice. From time to time I acted as Junior Tax Counsel to BP, when I was briefed by a young solicitor called David Steel (not the politician). Little did I think at that time that twenty years later Sir David would have become Chairman of BP and that I would have been appointed a Government Director.

It was while I was still practising at the Bar that I was offered my first very modest step up the political ladder – as Parliamentary Private Secretary to Geordie Ward who was Under-Secretary of State for Air. The position was one of the least onerous that I could have been offered. It took up very little time and, because it was unpaid, I could continue at the Bar.

Geordie was a delightful and popular man whose only object in life was to further the cause of the RAF. I have to admit, however, that he was a very, very poor debater. Fortunately there was rarely more than one full day's debate each year, on the Air Estimates. Normally the Secretary of State would have opened the debate and it would have been wound up by the Under-Secretary, but because the Secretary of State (Viscount de L'Isle) was in the Lords Geordie had to make both speeches.

Much is written about the rancour between the two sides of the House, but here we have an example of a different kind. Geordie's shadow on the Labour front bench was Geoffrey de Freitas. He had held the same position – Under-Secretary of State for Air – in the Attlee Government and, like Geordie, he too had the interests of the RAF at heart. So, in order not to expose Geordie's inadequacy at the Despatch Box, Geoffrey would give me, before the winding up speech, a list of the awkward questions which he intended to ask. I would find out the answers from the officials and at the end of the debate everybody would gather round to congratulate Geordie on his masterly performance.

As my practice at the Tax Bar grew and I became more involved with the political scene, I knew that the time was fast approaching when I would have to make a decision. The type of client I dealt with at the Tax Bar was not in the least impressed by my being an MP. All he wanted was sound advice and he frequently wanted it quickly. But if I could not go on pursuing the two careers in double harness, I was loath to give up the Bar because it was going so well and, in any event, it was the law which would provide the bread and butter in the event of my losing Doncaster – something which was bound to happen sooner or later.

I pondered long and hard the various alternatives. Maybe I could give up the Bar for the time being and then, maybe if circumstances changed, take it up again later? But that would mean starting to build up a practice all over again. Then there was another factor. It may seem presumptuous for one who was not even a junior minister, but I felt in my bones that, if only I could hold on to Doncaster, I could make a success of a career in politics.

As it happened, I was soon forced to make the choice. I was invited to become a Government Whip and, not surprisingly, I accepted this further step up the political ladder. And so, for the next couple of years, I sat on the Government front bench, learning much about the Parliamentary Party and the procedures of the House of Commons.

There is one interesting feature of the Conservative Whips' Office which is perhaps not generally known. Certainly in my day – and I think it still applies – when somebody new was being considered for the office, he had to have the approval of all the existing members. In other words, rather like a select club, one blackball excluded. This system, though hardly democratic, has the inestimable advantage of ensuring complete trust and confidence among a group of men who, together, know more than most about the virtues and vices of their fellow MPs.

Political gossip abounded in the Whips' Office and we enjoyed it to the full. Much discretion was called for. It was not an uncommon occurrence for a wife to telephone the Whips and ask if we could find her husband and get him to ring back. We could hardly explain that he was paired and engaged elsewhere than in the Palace of Westminster! Then there was the occasion when I was sailing with the House of Commons Yacht Club at Deauville and had to return urgently. The Channel was like a millpond, but when I returned to the Whips' Office, I found a message from one of my yachting friends who had also been asked to return which read simply: 'Regret unable to attend debate. Stormbound in Deauville.'

Of course there was the serious side to the working of the Whips' Office. No Parliamentary Party, particularly when in government, can function without an efficient organisation and a reasonable degree of discipline. There is nothing unreasonable in trying to persuade a backbencher to support the Government which he was elected to support. He is free to vote as he chooses, but if he frequently rebels against his party, he can hardly complain if he is not singled out for preferment. In fact, the Whips are far more tolerant than is sometimes supposed. If some aspect of government policy is particularly harmful to a member's constituency, it is well understood that he may wish to abstain or vote against the Government.

One of the most important functions of the Government Whips' Office is to ensure that ministers are fully aware of the views of the backbenchers. Early intelligence of opposition to some aspect of Government policy or of some incipient revolt can at least give the minister concerned the opportunity of talking to those who are discontented, and maybe the chance to modify the policy before it is set in concrete. During my time as Chancellor there were many occasions when trouble was averted by my being forewarned of the growing concern, often justified, of a group of backbenchers on some controversial issue. I might mention here that, as long as it does not occur too often, there are few actions that foster good relations between a minister and backbenchers more than occasionally bowing to a request and – very important – accepting with good grace the claim of the backbencher that he had caused the minister to change his mind.

By 1958 I was still in the Whips' Office and had been in the Commons for seven years. I was beginning to wonder whether I was ever likely to move on or whether, like some of my fellow Whips, I was destined to stay where I was. Then something wholly unexpected occurred. The Chief Whip took me on one side and told me that the Prime Minister, Harold Macmillan, would like me to became his Parliamentary Private Secretary. How it came about I shall never know because I had hardly ever spoken to the Prime Minister. But there it was. I was to have an office in No. 10 and the opportunity to see the operation of government from the very centre of affairs. I knew then that it was extremely unlikely that I would ever return to the Bar. So, with some sadness, I sold my wig and gown and my set of Law Reports.

The position of PPS to the Prime Minister was unpaid and, with my marginal seat, the future was by no means clear. However, there was something of a minor bonanza to help me on my way. In those days a retiring barrister had one valuable tax advantage. On his retirement from the Bar, all outstanding unpaid fees were tax free and, by good fortune, I had quite a few dilatory payers and hence some sizeable tax free sums owing to me.

10

Harold Macmillan

Life with Harold Macmillan was an experience never to be forgotten. As his PPS, he took me with him almost everywhere. Undoubtedly the most fascinating overseas visit was to the Soviet Union in 1959. It was a visit of great international significance, for Harold Macmillan was the first major Western statesman to visit the Soviet Union as the guest of Khrushchev and Bulganin.

Until the actual invitation arrived we did not know whether or not the visit was on. The Prime Minister sent for me and I can recollect the scene as clearly as if it were yesterday. He was sitting alone in the Cabinet Room and with an air of excitement in his voice he said: 'It's on. The invitation has come. You must come with us.' The forecast was for very cold weather and the word got around that the Prime Minister's party would be pleased to borrow any fur coats that were available. There were some magnificent specimens from the First World War, but the one which fitted me best happened to be the only one that was lined with mink. It belonged to Michael Adeane, the Queen's Private Secretary and, with its astrakhan collar, was much admired by the Russians!

A visit to Moscow these days may or may not be important but in the climate of the Cold War at the end of the fifties I do not think it is an exaggeration to say that the visit was regarded by the international community as a particularly bold move. That was certainly so if the media circus which followed us round the Soviet Union was anything to go by. As we flew lower over the Russian countryside, I watched Harold's expression. He did not want to talk or read. He was deep in contemplation of the significance of the visit which lay ahead.

On the evening of our arrival a banquet was held in his honour in the Kremlin and, not surprisingly, there was a succession of toasts. Khrushchev was well known for his drinking and what started as a rather formal occasion gradually became more and more convivial.

Harold was suffering from a cold and had a heavy programme ahead of him, and so started to drink his vodka half a glass at time. This was not what was expected of him and Khrushchev, pointing to his glass, made some remark which was translated by his interpreter: 'Mr Prime Minster, no heel tapping. Bottoms up!'

One of the problems of visiting the Soviet Union as the guests of the Soviets was the matter of security. There was no question of the Prime Minister staying with the British Ambassador. We were the guests of the Soviets and we travelled in their cars and we stayed in their accommodation. This meant that we were rightly conscious throughout the day that there was nowhere where we could count on having a private conversation. Even in those days the listening devices were very sophisticated and, whether you were walking in the garden or travelling in one of the Russian cars, you knew that somebody was listening. There was nothing that Harold would have liked more than to sit at the end of the day with a glass of whisky and to mull over the day's developments with Selwyn Lloyd, then Foreign Secretary. They both found it particularly irksome, day after day, to have to be constantly on their guard.

There was one place where we were assured that we could talk freely and that was in a remarkable room at the British Embassy. I say a 'remarkable room' because once inside you were in a contraption like a large tent with constant background noise as if there were hundreds of conversations taking place simultaneously. Was it a gramophone record? I remember Harold assuming that it was and saying that he would like to play it to the Cabinet when he got home!

Wherever we went the Russian people stared with curiosity but mostly in silence. After a while, Harold turned to me and said: 'Find out what I can say in Russian to these people when I meet them.' Before the next engagement I sought the advice of our Foreign Office interpreter, John Morgan, who many years later I was to meet again in South Korea. He suggested that he should say 'Dobrodyen', pronounced 'Dobrajin', which means 'Good day'. Harold practised the word once or twice and pronounced it perfectly.

Later that day he was confronted by another group of Russians and, with a sideways glance at me and with barely the flicker of a smile, he turned to them and in a clear voice called out, 'Double gin, double gin.' The effect was electric. They cheered and clapped.

On the following days, wherever we went, down to Kiev and up to Leningrad, he made his mark with 'Double gin.'

We travelled from Moscow to Leningrad in Khrushchev's personal train. It was quite an experience. The rolling stock was relatively new but the décor was pure Victoriana. We had already had a sumptuous dinner before we boarded the train to the accompaniment of a band on the platform. No sooner had we pulled out of the station than we were offered a second dinner served by immaculately turned out waiters with black ties.

I had my fill of caviar and vodka and went to bed. For a good night's sleep it was the perfect train. We travelled through the night at a constant speed of, I would guess, about forty miles an hour, never stopping until we pulled into the station at Leningrad at about 10 a.m., to be welcomed by yet another band.

If my time as Chancellor was the most demanding of the twenty-three years I spent in the Commons, those two years as the Prime Minister's Parliamentary Private Secretary were without doubt the most enjoyable. In later years, whether as Minister of Health or at the Treasury, those two years, during which I saw at first hand the inside working of No. 10, proved to be invaluable.

But life with Harold Macmillan was not just interesting. It was fun. We organised a series of tours which became known as 'Meet the People' tours. Some weeks before a proposed visit, I would go to the area with Tony Garner from Conservative Central Office and, together, we would plan the details. One such visit was to the North East and involved an overnight stay in Sunderland. The 'posh' hotel was outside the town but I thought it more appropriate for the Prime Minister and Dorothy to stay at a somewhat less salubrious hotel in the main street. The manager was thrilled when I told him what we had in mind.

The great day arrived and the suite which we had selected for the Prime Minister had been newly painted as the pungent smell bore witness. We had a big public meeting that evening and Harold never ate very much before making a major speech. The head waiter (now wearing white gloves) arrived in the suite to inquire what the Prime Minister would like for dinner. 'What is your pleasure, Prime Minister?' he asked. To his astonishment, the Prime Minister replied that he would like a boiled egg.

As we travelled round the country the local Conservative Association would be asked to arrange a reception for the Prime

Minister to meet the party workers. They were called 'receptions', but there was nothing grand about them. There was generally a cash bar and, importantly, there was no press. When the time came to leave, the most the assembled party faithful would expect from the Prime Minister would be a few words of thanks. Those were the circumstances which led to some of his best speeches – no press and no great expectation.

A modest glass of whisky always helped on any informal off-the-record occasion. One such occasion was a dinner of Church leaders arranged by the Member for Wimbledon, Sir Cyril Black. I am almost certain that Sir Cyril was a member of the Band of Hope but, be that as it may, he was a strict teetotaller and, somewhat irreverently, he was dubbed by some as 'PPS to God'. The dinner was held at the old St Stephen's Club which was on the division bell. We had a choice of orange cordial or sparkling water, and I could sense that this was not to Harold's liking. Fortunately, a division was called and we walked over to vote. On the way back he said that he just wanted to call in at his room in the House. The reason soon became apparent. We had a quick nip of whisky from the cupboard where a supply was always available and then returned to the dinner refreshed. The Prime Minister hit just the right note in a wide-ranging speech on the subject of morality and politics.

The Prime Minister's constant farewell to the crowds who came to see him was to say, in his somewhat patrician manner, 'Good luck to you all.' On one occasion, as we travelled down on the night sleeper from Newcastle to King's Cross, I realised that we were approaching the station at Doncaster, my constituency. I had not gone to bed but was having a quiet drink with Jane Parsons, a secretary from No. 10 and a Special Branch man. As we rattled through Doncaster Station I pulled down the window in the corridor and shouted at the top of my voice, 'Good luck to you all.' To my intense embarrassment, Dorothy Macmillan came out of her compartment in her nightdress, saw me and said 'Do find out who is making that ridiculous noise and tell him to stop it.'

One of the functions of the Prime Minister's Parliamentary Private Secretary is to foster good relations with the backbenchers. I had already had some experience of this as a Government Whip, but came to the conclusion that something much more systematic was required. I therefore got a complete list of all the Conservative backbenchers and, over a period, devised for each one of them some form of contact with the Prime Minister. If the backbencher had made a passably good speech which the Prime Minister had not heard, I would arrange for him to glance at the speech or a summary which I had prepared and get him to sign a note complimenting the backbencher. A personal note from the Prime Minister could engender enough goodwill to last for at least six months! And so I ticked off one more. Then I might seek out another member to have a word in the voting lobby, having forewarned the Prime Minister of some particular matter of concern to the member. If there was no other ploy, I might arrange for the member to be photographed having a talk with the Prime Minister. All this may sound somewhat contrived and artificial, but one thing every minister (including the Prime Minister) realises sooner or later is that, when he finds himself in trouble, he needs friends.

Harold Macmillan was in every way a rounded man who had thought through the ideals that governed his actions. To understand him, and his sense of history, one has only to consider the enormous changes which had taken place during his lifetime. I remember taking part in a Radio 4 programme and being struck by this short passage in which he encompassed those changes:

> The particular period in which I have lived is one of the most extraordinary in the world's history. I was born as a child in the Victorian age, with all its solidity, its sense of security, and I've lived through two wars, intervals of war, and seen perhaps the greatest revolution in the world; in the balance of power, in the relative strength of countries; in the life of the peoples, that there's ever been, perhaps since the fall of the Roman Empire.

Macmillan was amused by the many backbenchers who expected to become junior ministers almost as soon as they entered the Commons. He had spent many years on the backbenches before becoming a minister himself – time for reflection. Then there was the personal experience of the 1914–18 war, and the heavy unemployment in his first constituency of Stockton-on-Tees – these were the influences which moulded his attitude to life and his political philosophy. Of all the political heavyweights with whom I worked, none inspired more devotion than Harold Macmillan.

Although later on, when he dismissed one third of his Cabinet on the so-called 'Night of the Long Knives', it seemed that he was losing his touch, in those earlier days he certainly lived up to his public image of 'Mac the unflappable'. It was in keeping that he should have written in his own hand a 'notice' which was pinned on the inside of the door which leads from the private secretaries' room to the Cabinet room. It read: 'Quiet, calm deliberation disentangles every knot.'

I suppose that it was because I had such a high regard and affection for Harold Macmillan that I found the developing Profumo affair so depressing. Looking back, it seems to me incredible that what happened should have had such a grievous effect on the latter part of his political career. Like everyone else with an ear to the ground, I was well aware of the gossip and I remember one Thursday evening coming home and saying that I now had no doubt that the rumours about Profumo were true. I can pinpoint that Thursday evening as 21 March 1963 because it was the day before Profumo made his personal statement to the Commons.

I rarely went to the House on a Friday, because Friday was generally the day allocated to private members' business. For some reason I was in the House on that particular Friday morning and I heard that Profumo was going to make a personal statement at 11 a.m. I went into the Chamber and listened to him state, without equivocation, that there had been nothing improper in his acquaintance with Christine Keeler, and, furthermore, that he was prepared to issue writs for defamation against anyone who repeated the allegations. As is customary with a personal statement, it was heard without interruption and there was no reply or debate.

Am I more gullible than most? I don't know. What I do know is that, whereas the evening before I was convinced that the allegations were true, as I left the House that Friday morning I was quite sure that Profumo was speaking the truth. It was not so much that I found it difficult to believe that he would have lied when making a personal statement, which is a rather solemn occasion, but that he would be so naive as to deny something which, if true, would be bound in the end to come into the open.

When eventually the truth emerged, Macmillan was criticised for not having seen Profumo personally. Instead he accepted the advice of a group of senior ministers who had questioned Profumo, as it were, on his behalf. Among them was Martin Redmayne, the Chief

Whip, and Sir John Hobson, the Attorney-General. I knew Martin well from my time in the Whips' Office. A wartime brigadier, he was as likely as anyone I know to elicit the truth. And the Attorney-General was hardly the sort of person to be taken in by a mere denial. Also there were Iain Macleod and Bill Deedes. They were all convinced that he was telling the truth. I simply do not believe that, had Macmillan seen Profumo personally, he would have been any more likely to get at the truth. At all events, Macmillan took the perfectly reasonable view that, if the allegations were true, Profumo would be more inclined to admit them to a group of his contemporaries and friends than at a more formal meeting with the Prime Minister at No. 10.

There was one other factor which was on Macmillan's mind. The previous autumn another colleague in the Government, Tam Galbraith, who had been a minister at the Admiralty, had had in his private office an executive officer called Vassall, who turned out to be working for the Russians. A Judicial Inquiry completely vindicated Galbraith, but earlier Macmillan had accepted his resignation. There were those who thought that he should have stood by Galbraith and refused to accept his resignation. Macmillan himself regretted that he had not done so, and there is no doubt that this incident was in his mind when, the following year, he had to decide how to deal with the Profumo affair.

More recently John Major has been confronted with a number of cases where ministers have behaved in ways incompatible with their continuing membership of the Government. He has been accused of dithering and not taking firm action at an earlier stage. But if a minister denies any impropriety and assures the Prime Minster that the rumours are untrue, it must surely be right to stand by him unless and until the facts establish otherwise.

When eventually I ceased to be the Prime Minister's Parliamentary Private Secretary, he gave me the plum job of Economic Secretary to the Treasury. Thus I skipped the stage of being an Under-Secretary and moved straight up to the rank of Minister of State. Naturally I was delighted, but if Harold had wished it I would willingly have stayed on in the more lowly position of his PPS.

Five years later, when the General Election of 1964 was called, Harold Macmillan was no longer Prime Minister but he was still a great draw and he came to speak for me at my final election meeting in the old Doncaster Corn Exchange. The place was packed to capacity and from time to time scuffles broke out and the proceedings had to be temporarily halted. It was a good old-fashioned rowdy election meeting and Macmillan knew just how to handle it. He was no longer suffering the constraints of being Prime Minister and he spoke with virtually no notes. The old magic of the Supermac days had returned and he brought the house down. For some reason I had arranged for the speech to be taped, and I still have the tape. For those who remember him in his heyday I think that this extract is worth recording word for word just as he delivered it.

I say therefore, my message is very simple tonight. I'm thinking of a lot of people, young people, old people, middle-aged people, because we've had so many years when we've been able to make our country so much happier and better off than we ever dreamt of when I was young. We mustn't take it for granted, it's not something that nature gives us. It's not something which comes out of the sky. It comes out of the co-operation of a sound, sensible, energetic people with a wise government. It's hard to win prosperity but it's very easy to throw away. And I warn you, I warn you sincerely for I know how hard it's been to fight for this prosperity, I warn you that if you throw it away, it will take long, arduous efforts to restore it. That's my first message to you. My second is, no one has worked harder for peace, for some arrangement between the Soviet Communist Powers and the Western World. Sometimes in my efforts I've had to work against or rather at any rate without the full approval of some of the most powerful governments in the world. Britain is not of course in wealth or population, equal to Russia or the United States. But she has something to give. Something unique that comes from our history. That comes from centuries and generations of effort and triumph, comes from our knowledge and our experience, comes from what we can contribute in the search for peace; and I say to you, it will be a black day, when a British Prime Minister, whatever party he is, is told he is not wanted at these conferences because his country is no longer prepared to make the effort to keep it great.

II

The Treasury

It was October 1959 when Macmillan sent me to the Treasury. I spent the next four years there, first as Economic Secretary and then as Financial Secretary, and at that stage of my political career I could not have wished for anything better. My experience at the Tax Bar was particularly useful and stood me in good stead when steering successive Finance Bills through the Commons.

It was while I was Economic Secretary, and responsible for the excise duties on spirits, that we spent a short holiday on the island of Benbecula in the Outer Hebrides. For a complete escape from the sophistication of city life I can think of nothing better, but that is by the way. When I booked our room in the small hotel I wrote on my private notepaper and so, as we had hoped, nobody knew that I was a member of the Government. South of Benbecula lies South Uist and a little further south are the islands of Eriskay and Barra. I inquired one morning whether there was any way in which we could see a little more of the Outer Isles. When we came back in the evening we were told that the local doctor would be very happy to take us 'on his rounds'.

We travelled in a small boat with an outboard motor and, on our way home shortly after leaving Barra, we saw a rather fine yacht at anchor. As we approached it we could see that there were two men in full diving gear. Intrigued, we moved closer. They greeted us and told us quite openly that they were bringing up whisky from the ship which had been wrecked during the war on its way to America with its cargo of a quarter of a million bottles of whisky – the story on which Compton Mackenzie's *Whisky Galore* was based. I was told that the ship (with the unfortunate name of SS *Politician*) had been blown up in an attempt to prevent further pillaging by the locals. Clearly the explosion had not been totally successful. We stayed for about twenty minutes and, just before we left, they gave me a bottle. I took a modest swig. It was most definitely not to my taste!

As we chugged away, they were still bringing up the bottles and I remembered that when the ship was wrecked in 1941, some of the islanders who had pillaged her were prosecuted and ended up in prison. So what about me? After all, I was the minister responsible for the excise duty on whisky. Was I guilty of theft? Or of being an accessory? Or of receiving stolen goods?

When I arrived back at the Treasury my private secretary was pleased that we had had a restful holiday and added: 'I don't know whether you know, but it was somewhere around where you were where that 'Whisky Galore' business took place.' 'Yes,' I replied, 'so they told me.'

Those four years at the Treasury gave me an insight into all the major departments. But after four years I was certainly hoping for a change. I was beginning to feel a little stale, covering much the same ground month after month. During those four years, I was to work with three successive Chancellors – Derick Heathcoat Amory, Selwyn Lloyd and Reggie Maudling – each of them easy to get on with but each with a very different personality.

Derick Heathcoat Amory was a minister of the old school. There were no gimmicks and, although he had a subtle sense of humour, his speeches were rather dull. I suspect that the very fact that there was nothing flamboyant about him contributed to the respect in which he was held on both sides of the House. He was a model of courtesy. There are occasions in the Commons, particularly at Question Time, when it is very easy for a well-briefed minister to mock some less-informed but well-meaning backbencher. To make a fool of an aggressive member of the Opposition front bench is fair game, but the one thing that the House does not like is the cocky minister who takes advantage of his position to deride some courteous backbencher who merely asks a not very sensible question.

One incident is worth recalling because it illustrates the care which a Treasury minister has to exercise in the run-up to the Budget. Derick called me in one day to say that he had a problem. He had just ordered a new car, and now realised that it would look very odd if it were to be delivered shortly before the Budget. Would people draw any conclusions about possible changes in the rate of Purchase Tax on cars? What was he to do? If he were now to cancel the order or defer delivery, a suspicious person might conclude that he had it in mind to reduce the rate of Purchase Tax. On the other hand, if he took delivery of the car, that same suspicious person might conclude that the rate of Purchase Tax was going up. There was only one thing to do – and that was nothing.

Selwyn Lloyd succeeded Derick in July 1960 and remained Chancellor for only two years. Whenever I think of Selwyn, I think of misfortune and courage. His marriage went wrong and there is no doubt in my mind that the way it happened was not only a blow to his pride but a source of great unhappiness. Then there was the Suez escapade where, quite apart from the immensely important issues with which he had to deal as Foreign Secretary, he was involved in some of the most bitter exchanges across the floor of the House. Suez was a turning point in our history and it left its mark on him.

Then there was the 'Night of the Long Knives' when, wholly unexpectedly, Selwyn was one of the casualties who was dropped from the Cabinet. This was a devastating blow to one who had had a distinguished career in politics. There was no more loyal member of the Cabinet, and he had every reason to assume that he enjoyed the full confidence of Macmillan, the Prime Minister.

Fortunately, that was not the end of the story, for Selwyn was later to be elected Speaker and, bearing in mind his past career, that was a remarkable tribute to the man. This is a significant point because, in general, a candidate for the office of Speaker would not have been in the forefront of party political controversy, yet here was a man who had been both Chancellor and Foreign Secretary and, furthermore, had been at the very centre of the Suez debacle. Selwyn became Speaker because he was a genuine House of Commons man and because he was almost universally liked and respected.

When a member is elected to the office of Speaker, he has to give up all his party affiliations and I cannot think that it is much of a life for a man without a wife. I continued to see Selwyn and from time to time I would join him – just the two of us – for a quick dinner in his apartment before he donned his wig and gown and returned to the Chamber to take the chair for the wind-up speeches. He was a lonely man.

I should mention one episode when I put my foot in it well and truly. Charles Hill (of 'Radio Doctor' fame) was the Minister of Housing and Local Government and, because he was such a good communicator, Macmillan had also put him in charge of the presentation and co-ordination of Government policy, in addition to his responsibilities as the Local Government Minister. After a while he found the two jobs too great a burden and asked Macmillan whether he could have me to help him. Macmillan agreed and an announcement was duly made.

Soon after, Charles Hill asked me to take one of the weekly meetings of the lobby correspondents. These are meetings where the lobby correspondents are given helpful background information and, as I was at that time Economic Secretary, I made some rather upbeat remarks about the state of the economy. It was the first time that I had taken the weekly lobby meeting and the following morning my inexperience was manifest for all to see. On the front page of *The Times*, the *Financial Times* and the *Daily Telegraph*, the lead story was an unattributable account of the remarkable way in which the economic recovery was proceeding. I entered the Treasury that morning with my head held low and went straight in to see Selwyn and to apologise. The Chancellor looked up and, with a wry smile, remarked that he was very pleased to learn how well we were doing.

The third Chancellor I worked with was Reggie Maudling. He, too, stayed only a little over two years. I was now Financial Secretary, my position as Economic Secretary having been taken by Edward Du Cann. Reggie appeared to have the capacity to master any problem which came before him with extraordinary ease but he was no orator. This was very evident at the time of the memorable Party Conference in October 1963 when Macmillan resigned as Prime Minister. Reggie was among those few who were in the running for the ultimate prize and the speech which he was to make to the Conference was obviously of major importance. What was wanted was a speech which would fire the enthusiasm of the faithful. He asked Edward and me to look over the speech and to let him have any ideas.

We both came to the same conclusion. It might have done for the opening speech in a Commons debate on the economy, but the fact was that it had none of the punch which was necessary for a rousing Party Conference speech. So Edward and I spent the evening revising it and the following morning we went back to Reggie with our redraft. He read it through and said engagingly, 'It's fine, but it's just not my style. The fact is that I can't deliver that sort of speech.' If that was how he felt, he was quite right not to use it, for how many times has one listened with embarrassment to a carefully crafted speech which was obviously out of character with the speaker? As Edward Du Cann and I had predicted, the speech was not a success.

Meanwhile, Harold Macmillan was in King Edward VII Hospital and I called to see him. I suppose that it was because I had been close to him as his PPS that he discussed with me the merits of the various contenders to succeed him. It would hardly be appropriate to repeat all he said but when he was extolling the advantages of Quintin Hailsham, I remember saying something to the effect that, while he undoubtedly had all the qualities to provide inspiring leadership, was he not somewhat unpredictable? Harold replied that you could rely on the Civil Service and the Cabinet to deal with that.

12

Ted Heath and Margaret Thatcher

I have mentioned the importance in the House of Commons of having friends to whom you can look for support when the going gets rough. Harold Macmillan understood this and I am sure that Ted Heath also understood it, but with a difference. Whereas to Harold Macmillan the cultivation of one's political supporters was all part of the game, Ted seemed to find it distasteful to be pleasant to those he did not respect. Maybe he was right, for there is often something slightly hypocritical about political alliances. One other thing should be said about Ted Heath. For three years at the end of the sixties I was Chairman of the Party, Willie Whitelaw was Chief Whip and Jim Prior was the Parliamentary Private Secretary. We were all devoted to Ted although he was not the easiest of leaders to 'sell'. But to his friends he was 100% reliable.

Some of Margaret Thatcher's ministers used to complain that she would let it be known to the media that she differed from them in some important respect. The inevitable consequence was that they, in their turn, could not see why they should not make their views known if they differed from hers. During my years as Chancellor, although from time to time we had our differences, particularly over public expenditure, I knew that Ted would never arrange for the press to be 'tipped off' behind my back and he knew that he could equally rely on me.

It is illuminating to look back on the situation concerning Margaret Thatcher's economic adviser, Sir Alan Walters, which led to Nigel Lawson's resignation. Certainly if Ted Heath had insisted on retaining an adviser who was known publicly to be opposed to my economic policy, I would not have stayed. But it is inconceivable that the situation could have arisen with Ted. From time to time he would naturally receive economic advice from various quarters but he was always meticulous in arranging for his private secretary to send me a note regarding anything of significance.

The Duke of Wellington was reputed to have said after taking his first Cabinet meeting: 'It was a most extraordinary experience. I told them what I was going to do, and they started discussing it.' One reason why there were no resignations from Ted's Cabinet was because he always allowed a full discussion on any major issue which was controversial. Whatever the result, ministers could not complain that they had not had a proper opportunity to put their case.

Ted Heath will always be associated with the decision to join the EEC. If I have no doubt that we were right to join, that is no reason for not admitting frankly that there are aspects of the European Union (as we must now call it) which I find irritating. I ask myself why I should have to put up with an unelected functionary like the President of the Commission pontificating about matters which are properly the concern not of the Commission, but of our own national administration? Then there is the gravy train for members of the European Parliament which shuttles, at enormous expense, between Brussels and Strasbourg. These are the sort of matters which loom large in the press and provide grist to the mill for the Eurosceptics; but of course they are of minor significance compared with the big issues.

Those who doubt the wisdom of our having joined the European Union should ask themselves the simple question: where would we be now if we had not joined? I concede that there are some who find a superficial attraction in the vision of 'this island race' going it alone, but it is an illusion to pretend that we could isolate ourselves from the European Union.

The economic advantages of our membership of the Union are overwhelming. Because to many industrialists outside the Union we are the most attractive country inside the Union, it is to the United Kingdom that the greater part of the inward investment has flowed. The European Union comprises the largest single market in the world, giving us direct access to 370 million consumers in Europe. It is unthinkable that we should be outside it. We would not only lose that inward investment but, in addition, many of our exports to the other countries of the Union (which now account for more than half our total exports) would have to surmount the external tariff of the Union.

Then there is the matter of our political influence in the world. There are some who would not mind if we were to lose this but, for many reasons, I do not count myself among them. To me it is self-evident that if we were outside the Union that is just what would happen. For reasons of history and sentiment we would still maintain close ties of friendship with the United States, but the hard fact is that it is largely because of our membership of the European Union that we still count in Washington.

The United Kingdom is in a unique position, being not only a member of the European Union, but also a member of the Commonwealth. I remember attending a meeting of the International Monetary Fund in Washington where the main topic was international monetary reform. In my speech I set out the five main objectives which I believed should govern a new international monetary system and on which future work should be based. If I had been speaking only on behalf of the United Kingdom I would no doubt have been given a respectful hearing. But I was in a position to carry much more weight. We had given a great deal of thought in the Treasury to the five objectives and, only a few weeks before the Washington meeting, I had taken the chair at a meeting of the ten European Finance Ministers. At the end of the meeting we had agreed those objectives. I next chaired the Annual Meeting of thirty Commonwealth Finance Ministers and, after a day and a half's discussion on that subject alone, we found ourselves in full agreement with those same objectives.

I was thus in the position to say this to the gathering of the World's Finance Ministers and Central Bank Governors: 'So more than forty countries – both industrialised and less-developed – representing 1000 million people and comprising half the world's trade are at one on the basic objectives.' So started a major exercise in monetary reform.

Although all the members of the Cabinet were committed to joining the EEC if we could get the right terms, I do not believe we would have joined without Ted's determination and resolve. Europe was, even in those days, a deeply divisive issue and, as the Government's popularity slumped, some were tempted to take the populist line that the terms were not good enough and that we should withdraw from the negotiations and 'stand on our own feet'. By joining the EEC the course of British history was fundamentally changed and it is no exaggeration to say that that change was brought about primarily through the perseverance of one man.

Before I leave the matter of the European Union, it is interesting to look back to the crucial debate which we had in October
1971 and to contrast the stance adopted by the Labour Party then
with their approach today. The negotiations had taken place and
the time had come for the House to reach a decision in principle
whether or not to join. The debate lasted for six days and at the end
there was a substantial majority in favour of joining. But what
was particularly interesting was not only the advice of the Labour
leadership to vote against the motion but the fact that they issued a
three-line whip. The Conservative Government allowed a free vote.

Every week each party sends to its members a confidential
document known as 'the Whip'. Because of the historic importance
of that particular debate in October 1971 I managed, by devious
means, to get hold of the Labour Whip and reproduce it in the
illustrations to this book together with the Conservative Whip for
the same week.

One aspect of Ted's conduct saddened me and that was his
attitude to Margaret Thatcher after she succeeded him as Leader of
the Party. Perhaps one could have anticipated his reaction. I say
that because such was the placing round the Cabinet table that I sat
between Quintin Hailsham and Alec Home, and almost directly
opposite the Prime Minister. Margaret sat on the same side as the
Prime Minister, so they could not normally see each other's expressions, whereas I could see both! I could understand Ted's hurt at
the way in which, after losing the Leadership, some of his erstwhile
colleagues, who owed their position to him, quickly abandoned
him when he was down. But whether he knew it or not, he gave the
country the impression that he was a bad loser. It was easy for me
to approach the situation differently because, unlike Ted, I had
decided to leave the Commons. Having been in the Whips' Office
and Chairman of the Party, and having enjoyed the support of
Conservative backbenchers when, as Chancellor, I had from time to
time introduced some pretty unpopular measures – all these factors
conditioned me to put loyalty to the Conservative Party high on my
list of virtues.

This explains why in 1974, when the Conservatives had lost the
General Election and Margaret Thatcher had been elected Leader, I
went to see her privately in her room at the Commons on the first
day after her election. I took the simple view that it was incumbent
upon the party to close ranks and stop bickering, and I told her

that, the party having lost the election, I would quite understand if she wanted to distance herself from some of the policies which we had been pursuing, even though she had been a member of the Cabinet throughout the whole of my time as Chancellor. Of course I found it personally galling to listen to some of the extremists in the party rubbishing what I had been trying to achieve, but I vowed to keep quiet and not be provoked, and I have no doubt that, in the circumstances, it was the right thing to do.

How ironic it is that, when Margaret in turn lost the Leadership to John Major, it was not long before she began to make life difficult for him. She soon forgot (if she ever accepted it) that she lost the Leadership quite simply because the party in the Commons were convinced that she was going to lose the forthcoming election. They selected John Major because they believed that he was a winner and when the General Election came, they were proved right. The attitude of Ted and Margaret to their respective successors was nicely illustrated in a cartoon which showed Margaret looking in the mirror. And what did she see? Ted Heath!

With Margaret's convictions, it would have been quite unrealistic to expect her to maintain a dignified silence on issues about which she felt strongly. But, while from time to time paying lip service to her support for John Major, she must have known full well that, in general, she was undermining his efforts. For me, Margaret's disloyalty to John Major leaves a particularly nasty taste for the simple reason that he was the very man she wanted to succeed her. He therefore had every reason to expect her understanding and support in times of difficulty, especially in the case of a Government with a tiny majority.

But this is all 'small beer' when compared to her many achievements, and it is certain that Margaret Thatcher will be remembered as an outstanding peacetime Prime Minister.

A good example of her determination – even before she entered the House – is provided by her wish to become a tax lawyer. I have already mentioned that I was a member of the leading chambers specialising in taxation, and I well remember the head of chambers, Sir John Senter, talking to me about accepting Margaret as a pupil. Bear in mind that this was over forty years ago when there were few women with successful practices at the Bar, and none specialising in taxation. I am sure that John Senter never doubted her ability, but I know that he did wonder whether prejudice would prevent her getting the work. With almost any other woman, Senter would have made some excuse for declining to take her on. But Margaret was not 'any other woman'. She was Margaret Thatcher, and so she joined us at 6 King's Bench Walk. She did not stay with us for long and never built up a practice, but the time she spent learning the rudiments of tax law was later to stand her in good stead when she decided to challenge Ted Heath for the Leadership. It happened in this way.

After we went into Opposition in 1974, the Labour Government's Finance Bill was wending its way through the Committee Stage. Healey was Chancellor and Robert Carr was the Shadow Chancellor. Intelligent and courteous, Robert had been a successful Home Secretary but, in opposition against the 'bruiser' Healey, he was not in his element. There was another factor. One of the disadvantages of being in opposition is that generally you are not as well briefed as the Government. This is particularly so in the case of the highly technical provisions of parts of the Finance Bill. It is in dealing with this sort of issue that the Treasury Minister can so easily wrong-foot the unsuspecting amateur. I told Ted about Margaret's experience at the Tax Bar and suggested that she might be a match for Healey. So she joined the opposition team and, sure enough, she was very soon scoring points off the Chancellor. Her success did not go unnoticed.

It has been said that this was a mistake on Ted's part because it gave Margaret a chance to shine. But this is to misjudge Ted's motive, which was simply to strengthen the opposition Treasury team. Nevertheless, it is a fact that, by a stroke of good fortune – being given that opportunity by Ted – she considerably enhanced her chances of success when the chips were down and she stood against him for the Leadership.

It was about six months after the Leadership contest that Margaret went down to Birch Grove to lunch with Harold Macmillan. Harold's grandson, Alexander, recounts that she talked at length about foreign affairs and that Harold just nodded sagely. It was almost a monologue and it went on for over an hour. After she left, Harold turned to his grandson and said: 'Do you ever get the feeling you've just failed geography?'

13
Political Switchback

Political life is exciting, unpredictable and demanding. In October 1963 I had been made a Privy Councillor, given a seat in the Cabinet, been put in charge of one of the biggest-spending departments and, of course, was a Member of Parliament. A year later I had lost my seat, the Government had lost the election and within a couple of days I had cleared my desks at the Ministry of Health and in the House of Commons. I knew (or thought I knew) that that was the end of my political career. I was forty-four, married with two children, and it would obviously have been folly to commit myself to nursing the same constituency of Doncaster for maybe four more years, and then taking the chance that I might be returned again for the very same marginal seat. Even if I won it, the odds were that I would lose it again next time round. In the event, Doncaster was never held by a Conservative again.

In the weeks that followed the defeat of the Conservative Government, it was assumed by all concerned, including myself, that I had come to the end of my parliamentary career. It was the only realistic conclusion. If I had any lingering hopes, they were soon quelled by a surprising message from the Palace that the Queen had asked to see me to thank me for my service in Her Majesty's Government. No doubt she acted on advice, but I could not help thinking what a remarkable person she was even to consider such a gesture to someone who, after all, had been in the Cabinet for only one year. (As an aside, it is amusing to recall that I asked for an official car to take me to the Palace but was told that, as I was no longer a minister, it was regretted that a car could not be provided. I went by taxi.)

I reflected that I had been more fortunate than many of my contemporaries during those thirteen years in the House of Commons. I had had an enviably interesting series of positions – the Whips' Office where I learned all about the workings of the House,

my time in the Prime Minister's office where I had seen the operation of government from the very top, four years in the Treasury as
Economic Secretary and then as Financial Secretary, which gave me
a general overview of the various Departments of Government,
and, finally, that year in charge of the Ministry of Health.

I should say something about that year. It was October 1963, and
the day after Alec Home returned from the Palace as Prime Minister he telephoned me and asked me to take over from Enoch Powell
as Minister of Health with a seat in the Cabinet. After those four
years at the Treasury, grappling with the problem of public expenditure, there was something slightly ironic about my now taking
charge of one of the biggest of all the spending departments.

The next day I took my place in the Minister of Health's office on
the sixteenth floor of Alexander Fleming House. I had been told
that Enoch had prohibited smoking throughout the department.
On my desk were some papers concerning the organisation of the
department and a list of officials I might wish to see. A private
secretary entered and I asked him: 'Do you happen to have an
ashtray handy?' Like a good civil servant he had anticipated my
arrival and had one immediately to hand. We then talked about the
various senior officials in the department and, in the light of what
he told me about the first one who came to see me, I diffidently
offered this senior official a cigarette. He accepted it with a smile
and I heard afterwards that, when Enoch was not about, this distinguished civil servant used to repair to the loo for a quick puff. I
never smoked on public occasions or on television, but I never
pretended that I was a non-smoker.

I had only one year as Minister of Health, culminating in the
General Election, which was not at all satisfactory. In the first
place, the National Health Service is such a vast and complex
organisation that it is quite impossible to achieve anything of
consequence in one year, particularly when that year turned out to
be the final year of the Parliament. Furthermore, as soon as I took
over I was informed that many of the projects in the hospital
building programme had been under-costed. In those days the
hospital building programme was one of the great success stories of
the Government and yet, if we were to keep within the public
expenditure limits which had been agreed before I arrived, I had no
alternative but to announce the deferment of many projects which
had been expected to start on previously announced dates. The

NHS has always been politically sensitive and so, apart from the natural disappointment engendered by those announcements, they did not help the Government in the run-up to the Election.

Despite being the harbinger of such bad news, I got on very well with the medical profession. They had one thing in common with the members of my own profession. Both doctors and lawyers hold strong individual views and it is often difficult to get them to agree on a common course of action. This worked to my advantage on one occasion when a television programme was proposed in which I was to be confronted by twenty GPs who were to have the opportunity of cross-examining me and giving vent to their frustration, alleged to be the result of Government policy. The department contended that twenty GPs against one minister was unacceptable. I nevertheless went ahead with the programme and, with a few carefully prepared questions from me, the overriding impression of the programme was the inability of the GPs to agree amongst themselves!

This is a convenient place to mention one consequence of my short tenure at the Ministry of Health. Soon after I retired from political life I was invited to become Chairman of the Westminster Medical School. I had no hesitation in accepting. There had been a long association between the Palace of Westminster and Westminster Hospital, and many peers and members of the Commons had cause to be grateful for the dedication of the doctors and nurses. Then, almost a decade later, we joined with Charing Cross Medical School to form the Charing Cross and Westminster Medical School.

Ever since I became involved with medical education and the NHS I have been concerned at the seemingly endless succession of changes with which the professionals have to cope. Obviously no institution can stand still and there was much that was wrong with the Health Service. With infinite demand and finite resources those who object to the introduction of commercial disciplines in the NHS in order to obtain value for money are simply cutting down the number of patients who can be treated. Having said that, there must come a time when the reforms give way to a period of consolidation.

Minister of Health was the only Cabinet post that Enoch ever held and, in terms of practical achievement in government, his was a sad example of wasted talent. His political career illustrates the dilemma which sooner or later confronts every minister. No one doubts Enoch's intellectual integrity, but the fact is that if in the day-to-day running of government you are not prepared to meet your colleagues halfway you are simply not suited to a form of government based on the principle of collective responsibility. There are times when on a matter you consider to be of supreme importance resignation is an honourable course to take, as Enoch did when he resigned as a junior minister over the level of public expenditure. But the issue is not always clear cut.

Every Chancellor becomes frustrated with the problem of controlling public expenditure and every Chancellor, if he stays in office for any length of time, has usually at some stage contemplated resigning over that issue. I certainly did, but I eschewed resignation, not so much because it lets down one's colleagues but because it is rarely in the national interest to do so. After all, what is one doing? By resigning, one is simply announcing loud and clear to the whole world that the spenders have won the day. Hardly a satisfying achievement.

To revert to my predicament after the Conservatives lost the General Election in 1964 and I had lost my seat. I had decided quite firmly that I would not hawk myself round the various constituencies, but then I heard that Freddy Erroll (now Lord Erroll of Hale), best remembered as President of the Board of Trade, had decided to retire from politics and was giving up his seat in the Commons. So there was going to be a by-election in Altrincham and Sale which had a Conservative majority of more than 10,000.

The local Association would be looking for a new candidate who had the certainty of becoming the member. Not surprisingly, there were over 100 applicants for this plum seat, but I nevertheless decided just this once to throw my hat into the ring. I had a house in London and a family home in Yorkshire, so when the Selection Committee asked me whether I would be living in the constituency I felt in honour bound to say that I would not. The other candidates promised to move their home into the constituency. I knew then (or thought I knew) that the game was up. But once again I was wrong. Fortune was on my side. Soon I was the Member of Parliament for Altrincham and Sale, back on the front bench, but this time on the other side of the House.

There are some members who thrive in opposition, making their name by mocking the Government of the day, but, for most members, opposition is a frustrating time because only rarely do they have the opportunity of influencing events. Yet that is the reason why most of us enter Parliament. Ministers, with all the trappings of office, pose as statesmen and make authoritative statements every day. A party in opposition, on the other hand, is constantly being derided for not putting forward a credible alternative policy, but one of the greatest tactical follies that an opposition party can make is to succumb to the temptation to publish detailed policy statements too early in the lifetime of a Parliament. If they propose something attractive and sensible, the Government will have time enough to steal their clothes and introduce the policy themselves. If they propose something controversial the whole machinery of government can be mobilised to ridicule the policy as impracticable. Certainly an Opposition should prepare for government, but it is unwise to make policy pronouncements too soon before the impending General Election.

All too often the party in opposition appears to be indulging in carping negative criticism, and knockabout debate seems to be the order of the day. I remember leading the opposition attack on the Labour Government's bill to nationalise the steel industry. I picked my own team, almost all of whom eventually became ministers. Among them were Francis Pym, Nicholas Ridley, John Peyton, Patrick Jenkin, John Eden and Michael Alison. Some of the antics we employed to delay the passage of the Bill would not have found favour with the general public but I have to admit that we all enjoyed the exercise. We were ultimately bound to lose against the Labour majority but we had the somewhat frivolous satisfaction of mounting what was then the longest Committee stage in the history of Parliament. There were twelve of us and the Committee proceedings filled 2,590 columns of *Hansard*!

I began to get something of a reputation for aggressive debating but a politician in opposition should always remember that, if the tables are turned and he finds himself in government, he then wants to be taken seriously.

14
Chairman of the Party

In 1967 I became Chairman of the Conservative Party. To be Chairman when the party was in government would never have appealed to me. When the party is in office the place to be is in the Government, not running the party machine. But in opposition the office of Chairman assumes a different importance. Whereas – certainly in my day – shadow ministers operated on a shoestring, the Chairman of the Party is responsible for a country-wide organisation. During my time in the Whips' Office I had learnt how the House of Commons operated. Now, for the next three years, I was to involve myself with the voluntary workers throughout the country.

The funds available were limited and there was a limit to the number of speaking engagements that members of the Shadow Cabinet could undertake. The answer was to concentrate the effort on the fifty or so critical marginal seats which we had to hold or win in order to get a parliamentary majority. Among the seats with the largest Labour majorities, which we had no hope of winning, were to be found some of the most enthusiastic Conservative stalwarts fighting against impossible odds. They complained that we were abandoning them. Meanwhile, the safe Conservative seats castigated us for seemingly ignoring the 'true blue' grass roots support without which we could not win. Despite the pressure we did not waver.

As the General Election approached – indeed right up to polling day itself – the opinion polls were, almost without exception, predicting a Labour victory. Happily, they were proved wrong. On 18 June 1970 we were returned with a majority of thirty-one and Ted Heath became Prime Minister.

When the count was completed in my own constituency, I joined a group of supporters for a celebratory drink or two, and then flew back to London in an aircraft which I had been lent. On board was a bottle of champagne, which we consumed. As far as I can recall, we arrived at Conservative Central Office about three in the morning where a little more liquid refreshment was awaiting us. I was then escorted to the television studio in Central Office for an interview with Robin Day. Apparently at the last press conference before polling day, when all the polls were still against us, I had said, to the disbelief of the assembled media: 'I can say with my hand on my heart that I believe we are going to win.' In answer to a question from Robin Day, I referred to this and raised my hand to my chest. By this time I should clearly have been on my way home, for Robin Day replied: 'Mr Barber, your heart is on the other side.' That was the end of the interview.

Unlike the Chairman of the Labour Party, the Chairman of the Conservative Party is not elected and, although he is closely involved with the voluntary workers, he is not their Chairman. His correct title is 'Chairman of the Conservative Party Organisation' and he is appointed by the Leader of the Party to take charge of the party machine. In my day, he was unpaid. The fact that he is the nominee of the Leader ensures a degree of mutual confidence which might not prevail if he were elected by some outside body. Through a nationwide organisation the Chairman provides the link between Conservative Central Office and the voluntary workers throughout the country.

When I was appointed Chairman of the Party I took over from Edward Du Cann. I have already commented on what might be described as the unconventional political career of Enoch Powell. Edward Du Cann was a very different man from Enoch, but he was another example of someone who never reached the heights expected of him. We served together in the Treasury for a year. He was an able minister and a good Parliamentarian. He was a most popular Chairman of the Party, and for nine successive years he was elected by the backbenchers to be Chairman of the 1922 Committee. And yet, despite all this, he never made it to the Cabinet. It was typical of him that he showed no resentment when he handed over to me the plum job of Party Chairman.

Almost every weekend I visited one or more constituencies. If there is one prerequisite for the job of Chairman, it is that he should enjoy mixing with the party rank and file in the constituencies. That is not to say that there were not occasions when I was irritated by some self-important bore or when I was just counting the minutes before I was due to board the train back to London. But by and large my three years as Party Chairman were good years – particularly in retrospect, because they were crowned by a General Election victory.

There were three men in particular with whom I worked closely during my time at Conservative Central Office. Sir Michael Fraser, Deputy Chairman, who had previously headed the Conservative Research Department, fulfilled a role rather like that of a permanent secretary in a government department. He also acted as Secretary to the Shadow Cabinet and played a major part in the preparation of the Election Manifesto. Then there was Geoffrey Tucker who was Director of Communications. He was lent to us by Young and Rubicam (who topped up his salary to a figure which the party could not afford). Every day an announcement is made by one or more members of the Government and, because the Government has the power to implement change, what they say is news. The frustrating thing about opposition is that you can develop the most attractive package of policies, but you are powerless to put them to the test. Geoffrey had an extensive range of contacts in the media and advertising, and his primary task was to get our message across. Finally, there was John Cope, my personal assistant, who eventually entered the Commons and became a Minister in Northern Ireland. He was an invaluable aide with the rare facility of keeping everybody happy.

The showpiece was the Annual Conference which in opposition assumed a special importance. It was not only an occasion to 'rally the troops' and, one hoped, to see them return to their constituencies with renewed enthusiasm, but also an occasion for the party in opposition to set out its policies for the next Conservative Government.

A speech at the Party Conference has to be directed to two distinct audiences – the gathering of the Party faithful in the Conference Hall and the wider audience in the country, including those millions of uncommitted voters. A speech which will predictably ensure a standing ovation at the Conference will not necessarily influence the floating voter. I have to admit that one of the really exhilarating experiences in political life is to carry a great audience with you, culminating in a rousing crescendo of applause. Tempting, but not always wise.

It is sometimes said that the Conservative Conference is more of a highly organised set piece than a conference proper. There is some truth in this, but it can be overstated. Of course we wanted the Conference to go smoothly, but that is not to say that the representatives did not have the ability to influence policy. When we were in opposition after the war there was a Conference motion calling on the next Conservative Government to build 300,000 houses a year. It was passed with an overwhelming majority. It proved to be a vote-winner and, once in government, we achieved the target. But for the strength of feeling expressed at the Conference, I doubt whether that target of 300,000 would ever have been set.

Another instance, with which I was unhappily involved, concerned a motion to abolish a property tax known as 'Schedule A'. This was a tax on owner-occupied houses and was hardly compatible with the Conservative policy of encouraging home ownership. The Treasury line was that we could not afford to forgo the revenue and, as a junior Treasury minister at the time, I was put up to advise the Conference to reject the motion. I soon sensed that I was failing to persuade and, to my dismay but to the delight of the Conference, the motion was passed. As I left the platform, somewhat dejected at having failed, I heard a senior minister say: 'Absolutely marvellous! That's just what we wanted.' Needless to say, Schedule A was abolished soon after.

The selection of speakers from the floor, and the order in which they are called, are both crucial to holding the interest of the Conference. A succession of flat orthodox contributions can soon begin to empty the hall, particularly after lunch. In my day we had 'a little black book' with notes (probably defamatory) about possible speakers from the floor. If the debate was flagging, we would select someone whom we knew was likely to be controversial and stir things up. Conversely, if the Shadow minister who was to reply was a particularly dull speaker (and we had some), in order to give him a chance to shine, if only faintly, we would ensure that the speaker from the floor immediately preceding him was equally dull.

As Chairman of the Party I was responsible for organising the preparation of party political broadcasts. It was a task which I enjoyed, but I do wonder whether they are worthwhile. They involve a great deal of effort and expense, and, over a period, the advantages to the various parties tend to cancel themselves out. On the other hand, in relation to the total output of television programmes, the time allotted to party politicals is minuscule.

The Chairman of the party organisation is responsible only for England and Wales. Scotland has its own organisation, but occasionally I was invited to address a meeting north of the Border. I fervently hope that things have changed. In those days the organisation was abysmal and in certain areas virtually non-existent. No doubt the leaders of the party in Scotland at that time were dedicated men and women but it seemed to me to be somewhat unfortunate that many of them spoke with a pronounced English accent. It may be incongruous that in England the converse would not matter, but the Scots are a sensitive race.

One of my rare visits to Scotland was on the occasion of a by-election. They did not want me to take a public meeting, but to be filmed talking to people and answering questions as I walked down the street. However, some well- meaning but politically naive person had issued a notice stating precisely where the walk was to take place. It had not occurred to them that the Scottish Labour Party would be grateful for the information and do the obvious. They turned up in force at the appointed time and, as the Scottish Television news bore witness that evening, the Barber 'walkabout' was an unmitigated disaster.

Much is written about ambitious politicians climbing 'the greasy pole' and caring little for those who fail in the scramble to get to the top. In my experience, this picture of political life does not do justice to the overwhelming majority of members of the Commons, on both sides, who simply want to do a good job.

I am reminded of Harold Macmillan who told me of his disappointment after the Conservatives won the 1951 Election when Churchill asked him to be Minister of Housing and Local Government. After his exciting role in Churchill's wartime administration, the prospect of dealing with the minutiae of local government did not appeal to him. True, he got Churchill to agree to certain conditions but, as he said, in politics you should not ask for any particular position and you should accept what you are offered. It is an interesting reflection on my relationship with Ted Heath that, as Chairman during three years of very close working together, we never once discussed what position I might hold in the event of our winning the election. This is not to say that I did not think about it myself.

It is worthwhile remembering that, despite all the problems, during the whole period of the Heath Government from 1970 to

1974 there was not a single resignation from his Cabinet. No doubt this was partly due to the way Ted conducted affairs; but my general recollection is that we all went out of our way to maintain good relations with each other. To illustrate this particular point, I asked Willie Whitelaw to let me quote a Strictly Private and Confidential letter which he sent me from Stormont Castle on 26 November 1973, shortly before returning to London to become Secretary of State for Employment.

It was late November 1973 and the dispute with the NUM was worsening. The Government had declared a state of emergency, and a variety of stringent measures had been introduced to save electricity. In what was already a crucial situation, the Prime Minister concluded that Willie, who was then Secretary of State for Northern Ireland, should be brought home to become Secretary of State for Employment. This was his letter:

My dear Tony,

I had a long talk with Ted yesterday about my future and I want you to know from me one thing I said. I was ready of course to be Secretary of State for Employment but I insisted that in any briefing or any discussion I must be working under you on the economic front supporting your management of the economy. I must have no economic title or anything in any way which looks as if I was another agent of economic management outside the Treasury. I then went on to say that on the other hand if I was to work with you and support you I must have charge of the industrial relations activities of the nationalised industries rather than the sponsoring departments. In short Employment must become a positive Ministry seeking to avoid trouble and sell stage 3 rather than a passive and minor actor. I hope all this meets with your approval. I really think I can help you provided we follow the above prescription. I did also say I thought it would help all this if I were nominated as Deputy Chairman to you of Neddy.

Yours ever,

WILLIE

The fact that Willie took the trouble to pen that letter in his own hand at such a time illustrates his political sensitivity. It also helps to explain why he continued to play such an influential role for long after I had left the scene.

It is an understatement to say that politicians as a class are not highly regarded by the general public, and the reason is not far to seek. With some 651 members of the Commons, it is hardly surprising that there will be some who are stupid and some who are on the make, not to mention the occasional sexual deviant. All this is grist to the mill for the tabloid press. If I am asked whether I think that sections of the press sometimes go too far in delving into the personal lives of men and women in the news, my answer is yes. But if I am asked whether an individual politician should complain about his own treatment at the hands of the press, my answer would almost always be no. If you are not prepared to accept the rough with the smooth you should not have entered the world of politics in the first place.

There is another point. However unfair it may seem, you have to recognise that in selfishly pursuing your own chosen career you are inevitably exposing your family to a degree of attention by the media which they would not otherwise attract. I have known some members' wives who loathe the whole business of politics and just long for a quiet private life. There lies a sure recipe for trouble.

Of one thing I am certain. The worst thing any politician can do – and particularly a senior minister – is to hang on for too long. When I became Chancellor I knew that as long as I stayed at the Treasury I would always have to put the job first, but I was also determined that, when I had had enough, I would leave politics altogether. And that is what I eventually did.

15
Chancellor of the Exchequer

When we won the General Election in 1970, the Prime Minister offered me a choice – either to head one of the major departments or to lead the team negotiating our accession to the EEC. The former would undoubtedly have projected me much more into the political limelight but I chose the EEC because I recognised that here we were dealing with an issue with enormous political and economic consequences for the future of the United Kingdom. The Europeans could never quite understand why, when Ted Heath was conducting the previous negotiations, he held the office of 'Le Lord Privy Seal' and now here was I appearing as 'Le Chancelier du Duchy of Lancaster'! I was based in the Foreign Office and as the job was one that I had never considered I would be offered and which required, almost immediately, a number of important decisions, the choice of my Private Secretary was particularly important. I was well served by Crispin Tickell, who later became the British Permanent Representative to the United Nations and is the Warden of Green College, Oxford.

I might mention here a minor matter but one which illustrates the thoughtfulness of Alec Home. We set off for Luxembourg to make the formal application to join the EEC and, as Foreign Secretary, it was assumed by the media that he would deliver the speech on what was being billed as a historic occasion. Typical of Alec, he said that if I were to have the authority and standing to conduct the negotiations I should be the one to make the speech.

I knew that the existing members of the EEC would be listening intently for any hint of lack of enthusiasm. There was still a feeling in some parts of Europe that, despite the United Kingdom's expressed wish to join, supported by all three parties, we were not exactly wholehearted. But if I had to reassure our potential partners, it was also essential to sound a note of caution and to make it quite clear at the outset that there were some serious problems to be overcome and that, in particular, much would depend on the financial arrangements. In non-Foreign Office language, I wanted them to leave the meeting knowing that we were keen to join but not at any price. Translated into Foreign Office language, it emerged like this:

> After twenty years of political life, I can think of no greater challenge than to conduct these negotiations on behalf of Her Majesty's Government. I come new to the details of European affairs, but I have followed these matters for long enough to recognise, on the one hand, the great advantages for all of us if these negotiations succeed, but, on the other hand, our need to face up to the very real problems which, together, we shall have to solve. None of us in this room knows whether we shall succeed – whether we shall ultimately be able to agree upon terms which are mutually acceptable.

I went on to say that we had to find a financial solution which was fair, and I added:

> If I appear to labour this point, it is only because, unless such a solution is found, the burden on the United Kingdom could not be sustained and no British Government could contemplate joining.

Alas, after only a few weeks of savouring the high life of Brussels, my affair with the EEC came to an end. Jean and I were staying with our Ambassador in Brussels and I switched on the BBC seven o'clock news. Iain Macleod had died and I was being tipped to take over as Chancellor. And so it turned out to be – but not without a hitch which illustrates once again how fortuitous is the course of a political career.

What happened was this. Some time previously I had had an operation to remove a kidney stone and I had now developed another one which from time to time was causing great pain. Clearly in the light of the tragic death of Iain Macleod after only a few weeks in office, it would have been inconceivable to appoint a successor who might himself, at any moment, have to enter hospital. I knew that if the Prime Minister were to send for me and invite me to become Chancellor I should have to tell him the position and that would be the end of that. Then came a miracle. The day before the Prime Minister sent for me I passed the stone, the pain was ended and I never felt better. And so by a stroke of fortune I became Chancellor of the Exchequer from 1970 to 1974.

I was fortunate in having three excellent ministers to make up the Treasury team. Maurice Macmillan was Chief Secretary, Patrick Jenkin Financial Secretary and Terence Higgins Minister of State. Brendon Sewill, who had been Director of the Conservative Research Department for the previous five years, joined us as a special assistant. Although this was a political appointment, he and I took great care to ensure that there was complete trust between himself and the official Treasury.

For much of my time as Chancellor my PPS was Peter Blaker. An ex-Foreign Office professional, he was an ideal aide as well as being an agreeable companion. He is now in the Lords.

Because I had previously spent four years in the Treasury, first as Economic Secretary and then as Financial Secretary, I was quite familiar with the department. I also knew that the Chancellor is the one minister who more frequently than any other finds himself at odds with one or more of his colleagues. Every departmental minister naturally wants to be a success. The trouble is that to be a success more often than not costs money, and 'spending ministers' tend to support each other. The upshot is that from time to time the Chancellor tends to find himself in a minority. But it does not necessarily follow that he therefore fails to get his way. If the economic circumstances warrant it, the minority view of the Chancellor may well prevail because his colleagues recognise that, finally, he has the most direct responsibility for the public purse.

One striking instance I shall not forget, when, against my better judgement, I accepted the overwhelming view of the Cabinet. There was the distinct likelihood of an increase in the mortgage interest rate which, at the time, was a particularly sensitive issue. I had expressed the opinion that interest rates generally were likely to come down before too long and I was then asked by the Cabinet what would be the cost to the Exchequer of providing a temporary subsidy to hold down the rate for three months. The answer was £15 million. The Cabinet was almost unanimous in wanting to provide the subsidy. I was not particularly concerned about the cost of £15 million but, as a matter of principle, I considered it the height of folly to subsidise a particular interest rate. That was not what a Conservative Government should be doing. But my view did not prevail.

I warned the Cabinet that every serious commentator would be critical. Maybe I should have stood firm but I went along with my colleagues' proposal. It was decided that I should announce it in a statement to the House at 3.30 that afternoon. We worked on the statement throughout the lunch break and one of the private secretaries at No. 10 took the statement up to the Prime Minister who was hosting an official lunch. It came back with an additional sentence saying that the subsidy would be reviewed at the end of the three-month period. I felt that I had given way quite enough and I simply refused to agree to the addition. As I had predicted, we got a terrible press and, of course, it was assumed by everyone outside the official machine that the policy was mine.

Whatever criticisms may be levelled against the Treasury, one thing is certain. There is no Department of State where officials are more competent and more objective in the advice which they proffer to the Chancellor. The Treasury is also the smallest of all the principal Departments of State. I remember being told when I was Chancellor that there were more officials in the British Embassy in Washington than there were in the Treasury.

Because most issues have a financial aspect, it is inevitable that the Treasury should be involved with policy across the whole spectrum of government, and it is all too easy to become swamped with the sheer volume of paper. The danger for any minister is to get stuck in the rut of spending all his time and effort reacting to events and leaving himself with no time to sit back and ponder the longer term. Anyone who watched the series *Yes, Minister* knows that Jim Hacker's life was made impossible by the simple device of loading him with red boxes crammed with paper. One of the functions of the Chancellor's Principal Private Secretary is to avoid this by sifting the paper which pours into the office. He is always a high-flyer and Bill Ryrie was no exception. When he eventually left the Treasury, he moved to a top job with the World Bank.

Although I was familiar with the Treasury from my previous time in the department, that was some years previously and, because I had not expected to become Chancellor, I had not prepared myself at all for the job. The Chancellor in the outgoing Labour Government was Roy Jenkins, who by common consent had been a good Chancellor. I had been thrown in at the deep end and it is interesting to reflect that for the first few weeks Jenkins, a clever debater, got the better of me at Question Time. Then the tables turned and I had little difficulty in dealing with him. I had become au fait with all the current issues, I was better briefed and I had the advantage of the authority which comes from standing at the Despatch Box as Chancellor of the Exchequer.

I never really got on with Roy Jenkins. Perhaps the explanation is provided by this extract from the memoirs of Sir Donald McDougall, the Chief Economic Adviser to the Treasury: 'I got on very well with him [Tony Barber] – as I did with Roy Jenkins. Although highly intelligent, he did not perhaps possess the exceptional intelligence of Jenkins; but was in some ways a warmer character.'

We had two teenage daughters, Louise and Josephine, and Jean and I were not particularly keen to move into 11 Downing Street. However, quite apart from the security aspect, from the point of view of efficiency and the conduct of Treasury business it was essential. It also had one inestimable advantage – there was an internal communicating door between Nos 10 and 11 which was always unlocked. This meant that, unbeknown to the outside world and, more important, unbeknown to my Cabinet colleagues, I could see the Prime Minister at any time I wanted – provided only that he was free. A quiet word in the Prime Minister's ear before Cabinet could work wonders. It also meant that, if Ted had had a depressing day, he knew that he could always walk through to No. 11 and there would be awaiting him a bottle of his favourite malt.

So, in the summer of 1970, not suspecting we should be there until 1974, we settled into No. 11 which has been the Chancellor's official residence for nearly 200 years. It was furnished rather like a small embassy and, despite the fact that the vicissitudes of politics meant that my tenure might be short, we decided to surround ourselves with many of our own things, to give at least the semblance of 'home from home'. We stopped short, however, of replacing some rather fine paintings which were on loan from the National Gallery! In any event, we could hardly have discarded the portraits of Gladstone and Disraeli.

I recognised that it was essential to have a base available to move into when the time came to leave. On a change of government it is the usual practice for the retiring Chancellor to move out within a couple of days. The question, therefore, arose as to what I should do with our house in Knightsbridge. It would not do to let it on a normal tenancy for I had to be in a position to move back on twenty-four hours' notice. The answer was to find a very special person – a Conservative backbencher, with a houseproud wife, whose seat was sufficiently marginal that, if the Government were to lose the next General Election and I were to cease to be Chancellor, he would also lose his seat. I found just the man in Eric Cockeram, who had a majority of only 725. And sure enough, when we did lose the General Election in 1974, Eric Cockeram did lose his seat and, within twenty-four hours, he had moved out and we were back in our own home.

In those days there was no barrier to prevent the public from entering Downing Street. From time to time, demonstrations turned into quite ugly incidents. I remember one weekend in particular when the Prime Minister was away. A line of mounted police at the entrance to Downing Street failed to prevent some of the demonstrators getting through. Several police officers were quite badly hurt and brought into No. 10. The Metropolitan Police advised that the time had come to consider closing Downing Street to the general public. Ted Heath convened a meeting of what he called 'the Downing Street tenants' – from Nos 10, 11 and 12. It was decided that keeping Downing Street open to the public was a British tradition which should be maintained if at all possible. So it remained open for some years more until security considerations made it essential to close it. One consequence of allowing the public to congregate in Downing Street was that there was no privacy for those entering or leaving No. 11. Louise, who was then nineteen, was not enamoured of this arrangement and within a few weeks she had left to settle in less confined pastures.

Louise had already suffered one unfortunate instance of national publicity as a result of being the daughter of a politician. I was Chairman of the party at the time and it had been agreed that I should accept an invitation to visit South Africa. That was in 1970 when a visit to the land of apartheid by the Chairman of the Conservative Party was considered to be of some significance. My wife and I flew direct to Cape Town and, as I expected, the press were waiting to interview me. I was well prepared to answer the many questions about apartheid and relations between South Africa and the United Kingdom. But, to my astonishment, there was only one topic: 'Have you been told that, while you were in the air, your daughter has been arrested on a drugs charge?' Despite the important programme which had been arranged for us, there was only one thing to do. We took the next flight back to London.

Louise had been sharing a flat with two friends and the police, led by a certain Detective Sergeant Pilcher, had found a small amount of cannabis on the premises. She was fined £25. If that were all, the story would not be worth repeating; but that was not all.

At the time when the police arrived at the flat, Louise was out, attending a course at the Victoria and Albert Museum. On her return to the flat, she was immediately arrested and taken to the police station where she was charged. With a girl of nineteen that would not normally have been of the slightest interest to the media. But because she was the Conservative Party Chairman's daughter, the press and television were tipped off and were waiting for her when she was released.

Not surprisingly, it was on that night's television news and on the front pages next morning: 'Tory Chairman's Daughter on Drugs Charge'. But what really hurt was the account given by Detective Sergeant Pilcher in which he attributed to Louise some damaging remarks which she assured me absolutely she had never made. For her part, Louise wanted to tell the magistrate that Detective Sergeant Pilcher had said, among other things: 'That will get your father', but I knew that the reality was that the magistrate would be more likely to accept the word of the police. Perhaps those who read this account and do not know Louise may also be inclined to believe Detective Sergeant Pilcher. Suffice it to say that Detective Sergeant Norman Clement Pilcher was later found guilty of perjury and sentenced to four years in gaol.

There was another incident which shows how political life can impinge on the family. Josephine, our younger daughter, continued to live at No. 11, in a flat at the top of the house, and was working for her A Levels. One day my private secretary told me that the Permanent Secretary at the Home Office, Sir Philip Allen (now Lord Allen of Abbeydale), wished to see me. He came to my study in No. 11 and said that the Home Secretary had asked him to speak to me about a young man who was seeking to befriend Josephine. It transpired, from sources about which I need not elaborate, that the young man was a member of a cell with extreme revolutionary aims and was hardly the sort of person to welcome into the Downing Street complex. 'What do you think I ought to do?' I asked. 'If you trust your daughter, I should tell her what I have told you,' replied Sir Philip. I did just that. Nobody was more astonished than Josephine. The young man was never seen again.

No. 11 is a far more comfortable home than No. 10. The Prime Minister's residence has drawing rooms which are too grand for normal living and I always thought that the self-contained flat which is provided for the Prime Minister was a very second-rate apartment. The private apartments at No. 11 are on both the first and second floors and extend over the Chief Whip's office in No. 12. The rooms are both elegant and comfortable and have fine views across St James's Park and Horse Guards Parade. Our bedroom windows overlooked Horse Guards and one of my abiding memories is of being woken, early in the morning, to the sound of military bands rehearsing for the Trooping.

On the ground floor there is an official dining room and anteroom with its own kitchen so that the Chancellor can hold official lunches and dinners without impinging on the privacy of the private apartments. The Chancellor's study is also on the ground floor and in my day that was where we made the Budget broadcast. So there I was living with my family in one of the finest houses in London, paying neither rent nor rates. I believe that, later on, Denis Healey decided that some charge should be levied on the Chancellor for his accommodation. That was not a move that had ever occurred to me!

In 1973 Ted told me that he wanted me to become the first minister to reside at Chevening. With its library of 19,000 books, gardens and parkland, this magnificent house in Kent had been bequeathed to the nation by the 7th Earl Stanhope and was to be used by the Prime Minister or a Cabinet Minister or a descendant of King George VI as nominated by the Prime Minister.

Chevening is a far more beautiful house than Chequers, and I ought to have been grateful to the Prime Minister. But it was the last thing I wanted. We were already living in an official house at No. 11 and we had our own home in Yorkshire which I much preferred to visit when I could get away for a weekend, simply because it was my home. But the Prime Minister wanted to establish that whereas he had Chequers and the Foreign Secretary had Dorney Wood, in future Chevening should be for the Chancellor. In the end I reluctantly agreed and my photograph still hangs at Chevening as the first ministerial resident.

Then there was an unexpected development. I was working in

my room at the Treasury when my private secretary told me that the Chairman of the Board of Inland Revenue wanted to see me about a matter affecting my own personal taxation. His message was a simple one. There had been an oversight in the Chevening Estate Act and the result was that I, as the tenant of Chevening, was personally liable to income tax on the annual value of the whole estate.

What was to be done? There would have to be amending legislation which, if it were to exempt me, would have to be retrospective. Then, to compound my embarrassment, he said that what was proposed was a new clause in the current Finance Bill for which I was responsible. In brief, the Chancellor of the Exchequer was being advised to legislate to exempt himself from income tax and to do so retrospectively.

I spoke to the Prime Minister and he agreed that I could hand over the keys to Chevening to another minister which, much to my relief, I did – to Lord Hailsham.

16

The Vagaries of Office

Not long after I became Chancellor of the Exchequer we had a full-scale debate on the economy. As this involved one of my first major speeches since moving to the Treasury, it was important that I should perform well. It did not turn out quite as I had hoped.

I had prepared a forty-minute speech and I had also tried to anticipate all the interventions which I knew would inevitably be made in a heated debate. I had been speaking for about ten minutes and all was going well when Harold Wilson intervened and asked a question. This was just what I wanted. The question was one that I had anticipated and I had the perfect riposte. Remember that not so long ago he had been Prime Minister but was now Leader of the Opposition. In my overconfidence I made one stupid error. I leant across the Despatch Box to deliver my *coup de grâce* and replied: 'I will tell this to the Prime Minister . . .'

The Labour benches roared with derisive laughter at my gaffe. They stood up, pointed to Wilson and for what seemed like an eternity continued to chant, 'The Prime Minister, the Prime Minister!' I looked around in vain for some solace from my own benches and then turned to the new Prime Minister. Ted did not think it at all funny. His face was expressionless. It took me quite some time to get the speech back on track. To an outsider, such an episode in the middle of a serious debate may seem somewhat infantile, but that is the House of Commons.

When speaking at the Despatch Box you always have to be ready for the unexpected, but no one was prepared for the incident which occurred on one occasion when I was making a statement after returning from an EEC meeting in Brussels. The House was listening quietly to my report when suddenly, one after the other, two canisters were thrown from the Gallery. One of them landed at my feet and began to make a hissing noise. A voice from the Gallery shouted, 'How do you like that, you bastards? Now you know what it's like in Belfast.' It was in fact a canister of CS gas which can be quite devastating in an enclosed area. Robert Carr, the Home Secretary, was sitting on the front bench next to me and, when the second canister landed, he threw himself onto the floor between the table and the Bench. I jumped over him and ran out.

The only other comparable experience which affected me was when an IRA bomb blew up my secretary's office just off Westminster Hall. Most of the files were destroyed and at first Mary Lucas, my secretary, was almost in tears. But it soon dawned upon her that maybe there was some advantage in having a good clear out!

When unexpectedly I moved from the EEC negotiations to the Treasury I started with one particular disadvantage. Everybody, at home and overseas, knew that the Prime Minister's first choice for the job had been Iain Macleod. Iain was able, tough and had the reputation of being one of the best debaters on the Conservative front bench. How he would have fared after a few years as Chancellor, nobody will ever know: sadly, he died within weeks of taking office. For my part, I knew that although I had established a good reputation as Chairman of the party during the three years leading up to the 1970 victory, I now faced a different challenge. I had to make my mark as Chancellor, both on the home front and internationally. The two set-piece occasions when I could do this were the coming Spring Budget and the Annual Meetings of the International Monetary Fund and World Bank.

In October 1970 I announced some important changes of policy to save public expenditure and coupled this with a cut of 6d (2½p) in the standard rate of Income Tax to come into effect the following April. But I knew that the first major test would be the Spring Budget of 1971 and I decided very early on that this was to be an occasion for something more than just the normal annual affair. Instead, I would set out my stall for a full five-year Parliament.

I announced a whole series of far-reaching proposals for tax reform and simplification to encourage enterprise and savings, including the reform and unification of Income Tax and Surtax, the abolition of both Purchase Tax and Selective Employment Tax and their replacement by Value Added Tax, the reform of Corporation Tax and the simplification of Capital Gains Tax. In addition, there were immediate tax reductions to provide a stimulus to output and investment. All this and more, coupled with the substantial savings on public expenditure which I had previously announced, ensured that the package got almost universal approval in the press and an enthusiastic response from our own backbenchers. There were to be occasions in later years which were not so rewarding but in that spring of 1971, after eight months as Chancellor, I must admit that I felt that things were not going too badly. *The Times* seemed to think so too.

> Mr Barber today came out from beneath the shadow that had enveloped him since he took over as Chancellor of the Exchequer on the death of Mr Iain Macleod. His first Budget statement was a resounding success and the joyous Tory benches gave him a cheering, standing ovation as he sat down almost two hours to the dot from the moment that he rose for the most gruelling ordeal of his political career.
>
> Mr Barber's Budget held the interest of the House from beginning to end. The Chancellor might have expected a rough ride but except for a few left-wing mutterings, he was heard out in comparative silence.
>
> This was a most refreshingly new style of Budget, concentrating for its major news on what Mr Barber described as 'the most far-reaching reform of the tax system of this century' – and all to be completed within two years.
>
> As the statement ended, the delighted Tories trooped from the Chamber. Once again they felt they had a Chancellor of whom they could feel proud.

Among the many letters which I received from colleagues, there was one which, in retrospect, is particularly interesting. Keith Joseph played a major part in the reshaping of Conservative economic policy after the election defeat of 1974. Because this meant, of necessity, distancing himself from some aspects of the policy which we had been pursuing together in the Heath Government, it may come as a surprise that we saw eye to eye on many things. On this occasion he wrote:

> I write in admiration to congratulate you on your Budget triumph: the range of your preparations: the tactical handling of the strategic reforms: the great Budget speech: and the dextrous wind-up – all add up to a monumental achievement: when I consider the daily load on which all this has been

superimposed I marvel at what you have been able to do. And you maintained complete surprise! There was something theatrical in the stunned amazement and delight with which the Budget was greeted. You with Ted's backing have given the country a new chance. If the militants don't wreck our prospects your reform may be the start of a British miracle.

Those final words may evoke a hollow laugh today, but I would be less then human if I did not relish them at the time.

At the time of Suez I was in the Whips' Office and, as 'the Yorkshire Whip', had the responsibility for liaising with the other Yorkshire members, one of which was Keith. He and I were at one in being unhappy with the Suez enterprise but I took the view that, once the troops had landed, it was incumbent on all supporters of the Government not to rock the boat. It was my task to persuade Keith to take the same view.

As the years passed I got to know him very well and, during my time as Chancellor, I generally had his support on any matter of importance. That is not to say that he was not concerned at the way events seemed to be forcing us to adopt measures which we would not have considered at the beginning of the 1970–74 Parliament. I, for one, had stated unequivocally during the election campaign that we had no intention of introducing statutory control of incomes. When we did just that, we thought (rightly or wrongly) that the national interest demanded it. I do not argue the merits of what we did, but it is worth making three points. First, while commentators may scoff at a Government which makes a major U-turn, if you are in the driving seat it sometimes takes more courage to make that turn than to adhere to an election commitment. Secondly, although there were those who went along with the change with a heavy heart, it was a measure of the loyalty which Ted Heath inspired that the Cabinet presented a united front. Thirdly, those who now with the benefit of hindsight condemn the change of policy should at least take account of the wholly different circumstances of the early 1970s and, at least as important, of the climate of public opinion at that time.

It was the general view of the Cabinet – I believe that in this it reflected public opinion – that one million unemployed was both socially and politically unacceptable. We may have been wrong to introduce the statutory control of pay but the alternative of

attempting to force down the level of pay settlements by a programme of deflation, with the inevitable increase in the numbers
out of work, did not seem sensible in the circumstances of that
time. It is worth recalling that when we left office in March 1974
unemployment had been reduced to 584,000.

Most people assume that delivering the Budget speech is an ordeal. In fact that is not so, for a number of reasons. In the first place
the content of the speech has been the subject of exhaustive consideration over the previous weeks and the Chancellor is therefore
completely familiar with all the details. Moreover, there have been
many drafts before the final version is ready and it is accepted that
the Chancellor can read the speech from a full text. Then again, it is
traditional that the speech should not be interrupted except perhaps
for points of clarification from, generally, the Leader of the Opposition.

There was one occasion when the speech was somewhat longer
than usual and I had it typed on larger paper. After a light lunch at
No. 11 we were all set to step out of the front door to meet the
phalanx of photographers for the traditional pre-Budget photocall,
with the Chancellor holding aloft the red box containing the Budget
secrets. The box which the Chancellor uses on Budget Day is the
one that was used by Gladstone and is smaller than the current
ones. My private secretary was just about to put the speech into the
box when he realised that, because it was typed on larger paper, it
would not go into the box without being folded. Without warning
the door was opened and there were the ranks of photographers.
I held up the box in the customary fashion. We got excellent
coverage on television and most of the daily papers carried the
photograph. What only my private secretary and I knew was that
he had the speech and that the box was empty.

If the Budget speech itself is no great ordeal, what follows it is
certainly demanding. As soon as the Leader of the Opposition has
completed his reply, the Chancellor leaves and attends a private
meeting of Conservative backbenchers in Room 14 to speak again,
this time informally, and to answer questions. In my four years
as Chancellor I produced Budgets both popular and unpopular.
After a popular one the private meeting with the backbenchers is a
considerable morale booster. But it is after a Budget which is unpopular (albeit necessary) that the meeting in Room 14 assumes
greater importance. This is the one immediate opportunity, before

most of the backbenchers have been approached by the press, to attempt to explain to them the reasoning behind the proposals and to attempt to allay their concerns.

After that meeting there followed, in my day, a meeting with the overseas financial correspondents which, depending on the sensitivity of the foreign exchange markets, could be important. Fitted in at some point was the recording of the TV broadcast, after which there were also the inevitable phone calls to selected editors and correspondents.

The person who has the well-nigh impossible task is the Leader of the Opposition who follows the Chancellor. He or she is given no prior notice of what is in the Budget speech and yet is expected to make an immediate and intelligent response to the Chancellor. It is really a rather ridiculous custom which should be ended.

I have said that the Chancellor reads his speech from a full text. On other occasions, both in the House and outside, reading a speech word for word from a prepared text obviously tends to produce a somewhat uninspiring delivery. Churchill had the answer in a method of laying out speech notes which was known as 'psalm form'. I came across this when I was working at No. 10. The object is to lay out notes in a manner which allows you to have very full notes and yet, when delivering the speech, not to give the impression that you are reading it. It enables you to look up from the notes without losing your place when you look down again. There are certain rules. For instance, where possible a paragraph should end at the foot of a page. In no circumstances should a sentence be broken and continued on the following page. Each page should have a natural ending.

The following is an extract from what became known as the 'Wind of Change' speech made by Macmillan in South Africa. Here it is laid out in the ordinary way.

It is a basic principle of our modern Commonwealth that we respect each other's sovereignty in matters of internal policy. At the same time we must recognise that in this shrinking world in which we live today the internal policies of one nation may have effects outside it. In our own areas of responsibility we must each do what we think right. Our justice is rooted in the same soil as yours – in Christianity and in the rule of law as the basis of a free society.

Here is the same extract set our in Churchill's 'psalm form'. Any public speaker can appreciate the difference.

> It is a basic principle
>   of our modern Commonwealth
>
>   that we respect each other's sovereignty
>   in matters of internal policy.
>
> At the same time we must recognise
>   that in this shrinking world
>   in which we live today
>
>   the internal policies of one nation
>   may have effects outside it.
>
> In our own areas of responsibility
>   we must each do what we think right.
>
> Our justice is rooted
>   in the same soil as yours –
>
>   in Christianity
>   and in the rule of law
>   as the basis of a free society.

To revert to the matter of taxation. Undoubtedly the biggest change I made was the abolition of Purchase Tax and Selective Employment Tax and their replacement by Value Added Tax. This proved to be a mammoth task which was handled with consummate skill by Customs and Excise. After all, unlike the United States and many other countries, we had never had any form of sales tax, and here we were imposing a brand new administrative burden on the thousands of small traders who were reckoned to be the backbone of Conservative support.

I never had any doubt about the need for VAT. If we had not introduced this broadly based system of indirect taxation with its high yield, there would have been no possibility of making significant cuts in Income Tax. I would have preferred a uniform rate of 5% across the board on everything, with no exceptions, but we would never have got the Finance Bill through the Commons if we had included food, etc. So I brought it in at 10% with a number of broad exceptions. Why 10%? Primarily because it would yield the amount of revenue that I deemed necessary but also, which might have seemed somewhat frivolous if I had mentioned it at the time, because 10% would simplify the arithmetic for the shop-keeper having to operate this new tax. In fact this is a serious point because with any new tax it is important to keep the compliance costs as low as possible.

I have often been complimented by the media for expressly ex-empting books, newspapers and periodicals in the interest of the dissemination of information and knowledge. I am afraid that there was no such laudable motive. I simply wanted to get a good press!

As for the exemption of children's clothes and shoes, nothing could have been more ridiculous. After all, there are big girls and little women and there were many more deserving candidates for relief. But the tabloid press ran a most effective campaign and our backbenchers got the bit between their teeth. So I gracefully gave way and got much credit for doing what I knew to be wrong.

One further point about the several Budgets which I introduced. Although the state of the economy and the way it should be handled were the subject of much discussion, the actual Budget proposals were treated quite differently. If I had a proposal which significantly affected the responsibility of a particular minister, I would consult him on a one-to-one basis; but, apart from these comparatively few instances, the only minister outside the Treasury with whom I discussed the whole Budget and to whom I sent the later drafts was the Prime Minister.

The first occasion on which I would outline the whole Budget to the Cabinet would be at a special meeting the day before Budget Day. This procedure meant that, at that late stage, it was really not practicable to make a major change other than an alteration of rates. Such a procedure is open to criticism, but at least it had the merit of making it possible to produce a coherent strategy and to avoid a series of compromises.

I have said that I had to make my mark on the home front – particularly in the House of Commons – and internationally. Internationally, the major set piece for the gathering of the world's Finance Ministers, Central Bank Governors and commercial bankers is the Meeting of the International Monetary Fund and the World Bank which takes place in most years in Washington. Including the 'hangers on' there are some 5,000 people who turn up for the occasion. Commercial bankers vie with each other to provide the best hospitality and there is a seemingly endless series of receptions. But what appears on the surface to be one big jamboree has a serious side. It provides a rare opportunity for Finance Ministers to meet informally and completely privately.

So much for the social and informal side. The public proceedings consist of a succession of set speeches. This is not the place to dwell on technicalities. Suffice it to say that at the 1971 meeting I put forward in some detail proposals for a complete new world monetary system. The French, Italian and Japanese Finance Ministers followed me and each echoed support for the plan. The press could not have been better and, on my return, I received the following personal minute from the Prime Minister.

> It is evident not only from the Press and the telegrams but also from the comment which I have received from people who were there that your speech at the IMF was an outstanding success. One member of the audience told me that its effect was miraculous, and people seem to have been unanimous in their praise both for the matter and for the manner of it. There is evident pleasure at seeing a British Chancellor of the Exchequer once again taking and giving a clear, well thought out and definite lead in international monetary affairs. The political significance of this has not escaped notice.
>
> I send you my warmest congratulations on this great success; it is a great feather in your cap, and all your colleagues are enjoying the pleasure in basking in the reflected glory.

I had certainly achieved my objective of making my mark internationally, but did I deserve the praise? The fact is that both the concept and the detail were almost entirely the work of Treasury officials. As I told the Prime Minister, although I was involved throughout in the development of the new scheme, it was really the official Treasury which deserved the accolade. But maybe, on reflection, it was not so unreasonable for the Chancellor to accept the glory. As I learned in later years when things were not going so well and when, towards the end, we faced the most serious difficulties, it was the Chancellor who got the stick. Whether or not I deserved it then is best left to the judgement of others.

A Farewell to Politics

Throughout my time as Chancellor I enjoyed good relations with the City. That is not to say that they invariably approved of my policy, but I did take particular care to understand their point of view. I relied partly on successive Governors of the Bank of England to keep me informed but I also kept up direct personal contact with the leading institutions. There was never any embarrassment with the Bank about my talking directly with people in the City. This close liaison between the Chancellor and the City is important because the truth is that most ministers outside the Treasury have only a very superficial idea of how the City works, although they are familiar enough with its influence.

One consequence of this lack of understanding used to annoy me greatly. This was the frequent criticism of the City for allegedly failing to encourage investment in British industry. The fact is that no company is going to invest unless it believes, first, that there is likely to be a market for the additional output which the investment makes possible and, secondly, that it is going to achieve a reasonable return on that investment. It is nonsense to pretend that if these two prerequisites are not present, then somehow the City is to blame. What industrialists want is a sustained growth of demand and profitability. It is the responsibility of the Government to provide the right climate.

I have referred to relations between the Government and the Bank of England. It is important to recognise that the Bank is both forthright and independent in the views which it expresses privately to the Government and, quite apart from its views on general economic policy, the Bank is the acknowledged expert on the workings of the markets. The problem arises in its public posture. It is said by some, all too glibly, that any differences that may exist between the Government and the Bank should be expressed publicly. Unfortunately there is a tendency in some parts of the media always to be searching for some minor difference of accent and then to magnify it. I should add, however, that there are also occasions when the Chancellor of the day knows what is needed to be done but cannot, at that particular stage, get the immediate backing of the Cabinet; then a forthright statement by the Governor of the Bank of England can be just what the doctor ordered.

There are always pressures on the Government for more open discussion of economic policy and the provision of more information. In principle this is not unreasonable but life is not quite so simple. Who was it who said that it is difficult to make predictions – particularly about the future? There are some internal forecasts which, if published at a particular time, could be highly damaging to the national interest. To take one example. If the Government has an internal forecast which indicates a large increase in the rate of inflation, and if the Chancellor knows that he is going to take action in the very near future, I cannot believe that anyone would disagree that it would be folly to make public that forecast before he is ready to announce the action.

Because the Treasury has a hand in almost everything, through the control of public expenditure and the responsibility for taxation, the job of Chancellor is inevitably an exacting one. All Chancellors have therefore found it a refreshing relief to get out of the country and to meet other Finance Ministers who, in all probability, would be experiencing much the same problems. It may be difficult to imagine but, without our Prime Ministers breathing down our necks, and far away from all those selfish spending ministers, we can really be a very happy group!

Even the Japanese Finance Minister used to share the odd joke with me. Because his name was Aichi, and we were often seated in alphabetical order, we would find ourselves next to each other. On one occasion we were discussing the possibility of the more extensive use of Special Drawing Rights (or SDRs as they were generally known). It is not necessary to explain their purpose as an international money yardstick, but it was generally agreed that, to get away from the thought that the SDR was just some esoteric idea cooked up by international monetary theorists, it should be given a new and more meaningful name. Mr Aichi turned to me and said: 'Mr Barber, I think I have got the new name, but I am not going to tell anybody.' 'Why not?' I asked. 'Because', he said, 'I don't want to cause any additional problems for the British people. You see, I would rename it the "International Reserve Asset", but then everybody would call it the "IRA". Don't worry, I am not going to mention it to anyone.'

It was while I was Chancellor that George Shultz (US Secretary of the Treasury), Valéry Giscard d'Estaing (French Minister of Finance) and Helmut Schmidt (German Minister of Finance) and I formed the Library Group. Later it was joined by the Japanese Minister of Finance. It took its name from the fact that George suggested it during an informal gossip in the Library of the White House. The idea was that we would meet from time to time, without publicity, and that we would each have with us only one senior official.

One such meeting took place at the Château d'Artigny on the Loire. Each of us flew in, in secret, to a military airport and then travelled by car to the château where we spent the weekend together. I remember the occasion well. We sat at a round table and we all spoke English. To my surprise there was an interpreter present. Later on I asked Giscard whether we really needed him. Giscard agreed that we did not need him and I then remarked, with a straight face but with my tongue in my cheek, that this was supposed to be an informal gathering with no record being kept and that I had noticed that the interpreter had taken his notebook with him. Giscard replied, with an equally straight face, 'All right, Tony, if you wish it I will 'ave 'im shot.' That evening the poor interpreter appeared again at dinner. 'What is the interpreter doing here, Valéry?' I asked mischievously. Without hesitation, Giscard replied, "E is 'ere to translate the menu for George Shultz.'

Of the three Secretaries of the US Treasury who spanned my time as Chancellor, George Shultz was by far the most able. He had been Dean of the University of Chicago's Graduate School of Business and he retained some of the characteristics of academia. Listening to this intelligent, quietly spoken man, I sometimes reflected on one of the significant differences between the American form of government and that of the United Kingdom.

In the United Kingdom, the Chancellor of the Exchequer has to be a Member of the House of Commons. He has to fight and win a constituency. He has to be a competent performer in a debating chamber quite different from any other. Economic issues are at the centre of the party political divide, and if he allows himself to be knocked about at Question Time he will soon find himself in trouble. In the selection of the US Secretary of the Treasury, none of these prerequisites is relevant. The President can simply pick the best man for the job.

The Labour Government found a seat for Frank Cousins. He had been an able and powerful Trade Union leader but, when he moved straight into the Cabinet, he found that he simply could not cope with the House of Commons. The Conservatives found a seat for Sir John Davies, who had been an outstanding Director General of the CBI and was a first-class speaker, but he too was a failure when it came to dealing with the House of Commons.

If George Shultz was the most able of the US Secretaries of the Treasury with whom I dealt, John Connelly was the most amusing. He was the Texan senator who was in the car with Kennedy when he was assassinated. He laid no claim to any expertise on monetary or exchange rate policy but it was his turn to be chairman of the 'Group of Ten' leading industrialised countries when we met at the Smithsonian in Washington in December 1971. The purpose of the meeting, following the decision of the Americans to devalue the dollar, was to work out agreed changes in the exchange rates of the world's leading currencies – a formidable task which, for obvious reasons, had to be negotiated in secret.

At the end of one session I was walking out with Connelly and I remarked that the discussion we had been having was somewhat technical. He replied in his strong Texan accent: 'The truth is that I'm really just a cattleman.' In fact, he was a very astute chairman. When we all thought that we had finally agreed the package, the Italian Treasury Minister, a diminutive man called Signor Ferrari Aggradi, surprised us all by saying that he would have to consult his Prime Minister. Connelly turned to him and said: 'Well, Mr Ferrari Aggradi, there is always the telephone.'

Just before Christmas 1971 President Nixon and the British Prime Minister held a summit meeting in Bermuda. Connelly and I were summoned to take part and, in order to do the President proud, Ted had arranged for a grand dinner to be held in the President's honour on board a naval ship which had been ordered to Bermuda. Before dinner I had noticed John Connelly in earnest conversation with a certain Bermudan lady. As I accompanied him to dinner I remarked that I hoped he had been discreet in what he had said because I knew her to be very left wing. He replied: 'Tony,

I took one look at her necklace, I saw the word 'peace', and I said to myself, "John, you had better watch your step."'

On the few occasions when I saw Nixon I was immensely impressed. On one particular occasion I was invited with Alec Home to a small semi-working dinner at the White House. The discussions turned to the Middle East, a topic on which Alec was truly an expert through years of experience. But Nixon was just as impressive.

If most overseas visits were agreeable, there was one which most certainly was not. That was at the IMF meeting in Nairobi in the autumn of 1973. Before I left London I was concerned about certain ideas which were floating around and, to my surprise, while I was staying with Sir Anthony Duff, the High Commissioner, I received a message from No. 10 asking me to agree to a number of proposals. After much thought, I replied that I could not agree.

I assumed that that would be the end of the matter and, in any event, I was deeply involved in a whole series of important international discussions. One of those gatherings consisted of a working lunch which I was hosting at the British High Commissioner's residence for some of the world's leading Finance Ministers. We had barely sat down to lunch when I was handed a note saying that the Prime Minister would like to speak to me urgently. The timing could not have been more embarrassing or inconvenient but I apologised and went to the telephone. Ted had got my reply but would not accept it as my final word. I declined to change my mind. He then said that he would send out to Nairobi Sir Douglas Wass, a senior Treasury Official, to explain the position. I could hardly say that it would be a waste of his time. Douglas arrived the next day. I listened patiently to what he had to say, declined to budge and suggested that he take the opportunity to visit the local game park or have a night out on the town.

One of my most memorable days was Thursday, 22 June 1972. It had become clear during that day that we could not hold the parity of the pound without pouring in more reserves, which we were not prepared to do. So we were left with a stark choice – either to announce a straight devaluation or to float. I knew that floating was no panacea but, in the circumstances, I was convinced that it was the right thing to do.

Normally the Governor of the Bank of England would have been involved but Leslie O'Brien was on holiday in Cannes. We could not bring him home before the public announcement because the news that the Governor had cut short his holiday would have added yet more speculation to what was already developing into a crisis. So Leslie remained in Cannes.

In the early evening of that Thursday I walked over to No. 10 with Sir Douglas Allen, the Permanent Secretary, and Ted soon agreed that we should go ahead. I had explained that, to prevent a further run on the pound, we had to make the announcement before the opening of the markets the next morning, that messages had to be despatched throughout the world that night, and that there was much else to do. What about the Cabinet? After all, what we were proposing was a major change of policy. I explained that there simply was not time to get the approval of the Cabinet. Ted was at his most decisive. 'Go ahead and then get together as many members of the Cabinet as you can and tell them what we have done.' It was a measure of their trust that no one complained about not being consulted before the irrevocable decision had been taken.

The following day, being a Friday, the House would meet at 11 a.m. and I would make a statement. It was suggested by the Treasury that it would be courteous to let Harold Wilson know of our decision, in confidence, the night before. That would, of course, have given him plenty of time to prepare his onslaught on the statement which I was to make in the House the following morning. I declined the advice and, to give him less time, I arranged that someone should go round to his home and knock him up at 8 a.m. the next morning. How mean can you get? Incidentally, many unkind things have been said about Harold Wilson. I can only say that in any dealings which I had with him, I always found him courteous and straightforward.

The life of a politician is unpredictable and none more so than that of a Treasury Minister – for the simple reason that, despite the best laid domestic plans to achieve the goal of non-inflationary growth, it is impossible for the United Kingdom to isolate itself from developments elsewhere in the world and particularly from changes which take place in the economies of its major trading partners. That is why the Treasury always has continuously updated contingency plans to deal with possible external developments.

One of the most dramatic events during my time in politics was the decision by OPEC to quadruple the price of oil. It had enormous economic and political consequences, not only for the United Kingdom but for the world economy and particularly for the Third World. The banking system was soon to be awash with oil money which it then lent on to the developing countries. Now, with hindsight, the banks are criticised for the build up of Third World debt, but at the time very few commentators predicted the way things would turn out. As far as the United Kingdom was concerned, remember that this was before North Sea oil was available in commercial quantities.

The impact on the United Kingdom's balance of payments was clear for all to see. Prior to the fourfold hike in oil prices, I had from time to time warned my colleagues about the balance of payments, but often I could see from their reaction that they suspected that this was just the dreary Treasury at it again. But this time it was quite different. Any member of the Government could work out the increased cost of our oil imports on the back of an envelope, not to mention the effect on both domestic prices and the prices of our exports.

It was clear to me as Chancellor that the economic policy we had been pursuing would have to be radically changed to cope with an entirely new situation. I do not dwell on the merits of the policy which I had been pursuing, or the changes proposed, as these memoirs are not an exercise in self-justification. But it is interesting to trace the quite different ways of dealing with the situation by the outgoing Conservative Government and the new Labour Government following the General Election of February 1974.

I announced by far the largest reduction in public expenditure for a succeeding year which had ever been made, both in absolute and in relative terms. It meant curtailing or deferring a host of desirable projects to which we had been looking forward. If there were occasions in the past – and there were – when I failed to get my way on items of public expenditure, it is to the credit of the members of the Cabinet that, in this instance, I had their full backing for the deeply unpopular announcements which it was necessary to make.

The result was that, whereas public expenditure on goods and services had been expected to rise by nearly 3 per cent the following year, it would now fall by over 3 per cent, and whereas total public expenditure was expected to rise by under 2 per cent next year, it would now fall by some 2 per cent.

After the General Election, the new Labour Government reversed the trend and set about increasing public expenditure by 14 per cent in their first year of office. 'Res ipsa loquitur' as the lawyers say. 'The thing speaks for itself'.

Some two years before the February 1974 General Election I had told the Prime Minister that I wanted to retire from politics at the end of that Parliament. I have never had any regrets about that decision but I remember wondering what life would be like outside Parliament after almost a quarter of a century inside. Although I was naturally disappointed (but not surprised) that the Conservative Government should have been defeated, I had not anticipated the sudden sense of relief in no longer having to shoulder the burden of the Exchequer.

I was out of my room in the Treasury immediately, but Denis Healey, who succeeded me as Chancellor, and his wife were quite content that Jean and I should depart from No. 11 somewhat less hastily. I soon realised, however, that it would have been embarrassing not to leave soon. There was that open communicating door to No. 10 where Harold Wilson was now ensconced as Prime Minister. Then there was that kitchen window, which looked up Downing Street towards Whitehall. I could not resist watching the comings and goings next door of those who were to form the new Labour Government. So the removal van was quickly summoned and, to my surprise, some of the sightseers, who were still allowed in Downing Street in those days, were enjoying themselves taking photographs of our personal possessions as they were being loaded into the van!

Although I would have preferred to give up my seat in the Commons at that February election, it was obvious that there was no way in which I could announce such a move while I was Chancellor. I therefore kept my seat, and was a member of the Shadow Cabinet, until the next General Election which came in the autumn. Then I was not only free from the constraints of ministerial office but also no longer a Member of Parliament. No more Saturday afternoon 'surgeries'. There was the constituent who came to me for advice as to how to fill in one part of his Income Tax return. I was Chancellor of the Exchequer at the time. I politely declined, not because it would have been unwise to advise him, but because I could not understand it!

Never again, I thought with relish, would I have to take account of the electorate. I vowed that henceforth I would say what I had always wanted to say – to that insolent waiter, to that unhelpful shop assistant, to the morose ill-tempered official at the railway station. The truth was that I had become so accustomed to being 'nice' (except during debates in the House of Commons) that I found it difficult to get out of the habit.

Now I was not only free from the cares of office and the constituency, but soon I was to enjoy the growing anonymity which gradually comes to those who retire from politics, until the present day – twenty years on – when the closest I get to recognition was illustrated by the taxi driver who stared at me as I fumbled for a tip and said: 'Excuse me, sir, but are you Roy Plomley?'

18

A Lost Opportunity

On 28 February 1974 we lost the General Election, and one of my serious regrets is that, as a consequence, we did not have the opportunity to introduce the Tax Credit scheme – a scheme which would have revolutionised our taxation and social security systems. Before I explain its purpose and how we set about devising it, here is the commitment we made in the General Election manifesto:

> The centre-piece of our social programme will be the Tax Credit scheme – the most advanced anti-poverty programme set in hand by any western country. This scheme will provide cash help, related to family circumstances, automatically and without special means test. It will be of special help to pensioners and to hard-pressed families with low incomes, especially where there are children. Our intention is to ensure that ultimately no family in the land need remain in poverty. We will establish the framework for tax credits as soon as we can and bring the scheme into effect in stages, as economic circumstances permit.

The essence of the scheme was to bring together large parts of the taxation and social security systems. It is obvious that there is an area of overlap between the various tax allowances and the social security cash allowances. So why not, to as great an extent as practicable, merge the Income Tax system and the social security system? Many people in many countries have, over the years, been attracted to some form of 'negative Income Tax', as it is sometimes called. The theoretical attraction of such a system is that there should be a single assessment of income which would suffice either to calculate the tax due from the individual if his income is above a certain level or to calculate the social benefit to be paid out to him if it is below that level.

It was clear to me that if the concept of such a system could be translated into a scheme which would actually work, the advantages would be enormous. The prize was very great. Such a scheme would provide a fairer and more accurate method of directing help to many people in need. It would deal with the problem of the borderline between taxation and social benefits. It would also provide a smoother graduation from the area of benefit to that of taxation, and so avoid some of the worst features of the present system in its disincentive to earn more. From an economic point of view, this last point is important.

But it is one thing to subscribe to a principle, quite another to say how it would work in practice. One of the difficulties of making progress had always been that 'no really detailed scheme, which took account of all the complications of the twin systems of taxation and social security, and which could reasonably be regarded as practicable and acceptable, had ever been put forward as a basis for discussion.

What was needed therefore, was a system which would rationalise the two systems, avoid overlap and simplify them. The essential objective, it seemed to me, was a system under which the benefits would be available, so far as possible, automatically – without a separate test of means.

So, both from the point of view of further simplifying the tax system and from the point of view of merging the two areas of obvious overlap – taxation and social security – there seemed to be overwhelming reasons to press ahead with a real study of the possibilities. Of course there were problems; for instance, the two systems – taxation and social security – had evolved very differently. The set of reliefs and allowances embodied in the tax system was based on one set of principles. The social security system embodied a different set of benefits and allowances based on a different set of principles. Each had been amended and added to again and again over the years. It was not going to be easy to bring these two separate systems together into a simpler and more general system.

I had already learned from my experience with the other taxation reforms that in order to gain acceptance by both the tax pundits and the general public, two things were necessary. First, the details should, if possible, be worked out in complete confidence, so as to avoid premature and partial disclosure that would result in the proposed reforms going off at half-cock and then being open to ill-informed criticism. Secondly, once the draft proposals were published, they should be the subject of widespread consultation. And also – very important politically – one should not die in the last ditch to preserve what I might call the theoretical purity of a reform if public opinion is strongly against some particular aspect which is not basic.

The first step was a detailed scheme which was produced by Arthur Cockfield (now Lord Cockfield), my special adviser on taxation. Without his experience and inventive mind, the scheme would never have got off the ground. I should mention that, at that stage, the scheme had not been submitted to either the Inland Revenue or the Department of Social Security. I then began to realise that, at last, we were on to something which seemed to me to have all the makings of a practicable scheme and which could virtually revolutionise the systems of personal taxation and social security which had developed piecemeal over the years.

The next move was to submit the scheme to the critical consideration of the Departments of Inland Revenue and Social Security. So I set up a working group of senior officials from these two departments – some full time on this particular project – to examine the new system. Their studies confirmed my own belief that it was both practicable and desirable. So this was not just another bright idea. Those who would have to operate the new system in the two departments concerned were as enthusiastic as I was.

And all this time, while this work was going on, the whole subject was kept confidential. Apart from Keith Joseph, who was then Secretary of State for Social Services, I told only the Prime Minister. By the time of my March 1972 Budget I was ready to inform the House of Commons and to tell them that I proposed to produce a discussion paper setting out the scheme in detail. And I also suggested that the House of Commons should set up a special Select Committee to study the proposals in depth. The reason for proceeding in this way was because I wanted, if at all possible, to carry the whole House of Commons with me in such a radical change, and not simply to rely on the Government majority.

In the autumn of 1972 the discussion paper was duly published. It contained proposals which went further than I had thought possible when we first set out down this road. The proposed Tax Credit system would cover about ninety per cent of the British people. For all these people, the main tax allowances would be abolished altogether. Instead, they would receive a simple credit; a credit which would be payable whether or not the recipient was a tax payer.

These Tax Credits would be set off against any liability to tax. For those people whose credit was less than the tax payable the Inland Revenue would collect the difference. But where the credit was greater than any liability to tax, the difference would be paid out in cash as an addition to the income.

One of the real tests of rationalisation and simplification is: do you save any staff? Can you cut down the bureaucracy? So often new ideas produce more staff, and sometimes more complication. But in this case the scheme really would have produced savings – about 15,000 people in the Revenue and Social Security Departments – and both these departments were eager to go ahead.

We have, in Britain, a taxation system which, although far too involved and complex, is by and large fair. We also have a comprehensive social security system which, although open to abuse, caters for the overwhelming majority of cases where assistance of one kind or another is needed. The particular merit of the Tax Credit system is that it was devised and worked out, in great practical detail, as a co-operative effort between those responsible for the official machine and those – the academics and the social workers – who can sometimes take a broader view. Added to this it had the widespread support of the articulate general public. It seemed to me that the case for its introduction was unassailable.

And so, in the 1974 General Election Manifesto, we gave an absolute commitment to introduce the scheme. Unfortunately we lost the election and the incoming Labour Government, for reasons which frankly were quite spurious, decided to abandon the scheme. Thus it was that the opportunity to implement a major reform of our taxation and social security systems, which should have been above party politics, was lost.

19
Living with the Media

My relations with the media were almost always good, even though what they said was not always helpful. If it is in the interest of ministers to keep on good terms with the political and economic correspondents, it is equally in the correspondents' interests not to foul up relations with ministers. That is why, when dealing with good journalists whom you trust, there is no need to be continually saying 'This is off the record' or 'This is for background only'. They have enough nous to know what is not meant for publication or attribution.

In the sixties and seventies interviews with senior politicians were conducted with greater courtesy than today, but they were no less demanding. The prime objective of some present-day radio and TV interviewers seems to be to wrong-foot the person being interviewed by aggressive cross-examination. Generally speaking, I do not believe that they are any more effective at eliciting the truth than the likes of Robin Day. The one thing you always knew about Robin was that he had mastered every aspect of the topic under discussion.

One newspaper man whom I have known over many years is Sir John Junor. The longest-serving editor of the *Daily Express* and now a columnist, he encapsulates everything I associate with the words 'Fleet Street'. But because of the forthright way in which he expresses his often controversial views, some of my political friends tended to fight shy of him. To me, lunch with John Junor was always enjoyable.

I mention him for another particular reason. When I was living at No. 11 he asked me one day whether his daughter, Penny, could interview Josephine, our seventeen-year-old daughter, who was living with us and studying for her A levels. The result was a feature article in the London *Evening Standard*. It was, in fact, Penny Junor's first ever article to be published and John still has the payslip which he keeps as a memento of the beginning of his daughter's very successful career.

I always thought that the televising of Parliamentary proceedings was a mistake, but I supported it because I knew that it was inevitable. A full day's debate on the economy, from 3.30 p.m. to 10 p.m., may be at times tedious and repetitive but, be that as it may, it is representative of a day in the life of the Commons – very different from the impression given by watching a news report which understandably selects mainly controversial passages from the front bench speeches. Then there are Prime Minister's Questions. TV editors can hardly be blamed for highlighting these twice-weekly contests, even though they represent only one aspect of the day's proceedings. Nevertheless, I have to say that by and large the televising of Parliament is fairly presented. And one undoubted bonus is the recognition by the general public of the very high standard of debate in the House of Lords.

Soon after becoming Chancellor I realised that the Treasury's relations with the media left much to be desired. My friends in Fleet Street complained that the Treasury Press Office always seemed to be on the defensive and appeared hesitant even to provide information which was not in any way market sensitive. To be fair to the Press Office, or the 'Information Department' as I think it was called, the Treasury, unlike most other government departments, has much information that cannot be made public; and because some injudicious comment or aside could affect the markets, there was a natural tendency to play safe.

I came to the conclusion that we should adopt the Foreign Office practice. The senior Foreign Office spokesman is not a professional from the corps of information officers, but a rising diplomat who does the job for a period. The system has the double advantage of giving some budding ambassador the experience of dealing with the media and also of providing a spokesman who is well versed in what is going on. I had just the man in my private office. He was Peter Middleton, a good communicator, who had the advantage, as a private secretary, of having been involved with all the important issues of the day.

There was considerable opposition from the professional information officers, because they considered such a move a threat to their own careers. In the end I got my way and the new arrangement made all the difference. No longer did we appear to respond by stone-walling. In due course Peter Middleton became Permanent Secretary to the Treasury and I like to think that the experience which he gained and the contacts which he made in those earlier days stood him in good stead when he eventually became the senior Treasury official.

When I ceased to be Chancellor and was succeeded by Denis Healey, Peter Middleton immediately became his spokesman. You could hardly have a more striking example of the apolitical stance of the British Civil Service.

We are all receptive to a little flattery, journalists included. Ted Heath (then Leader of the Opposition), myself (Chairman of the party) and Chris Chataway (who was shadowing Overseas Aid) were on a tour of South East Asia and the Far East, accompanied by a contingent from the British press and television. In Malaysia we were guests of the then King, Tunku Abdul Rahman, and, although invited to meet the press, he declined to do so. It was not the style for the King of Malaysia. The next evening we were in Singapore where the Prime Minister, Lee Kuan Yew, went out of his way to speak to every single member of the media who were with us. The Tunku got a bad press, Lee Kuan Yew got a good one.

It was on that same tour of South East Asia that we travelled to Borneo to visit the British troops engaged in operations against a group of armed insurgents. The idea was to show the Leader of the Opposition as an international statesman of stature. Unfortunately, on one occasion things did not quite work out as intended. The TV crews who accompanied us wanted to get a shot of Ted landing by helicopter and being greeted by the troops in the middle of the Borneo jungle. It was all most carefully stage-managed. The TV crews were flown in first, and got their cameras set up for the great man's arrival. Alas, it all went wrong because we had with us one lady correspondent and Ted, being a gentleman, invited her to go first. And so, instead of the intrepid Heath setting foot in the dank infested jungle, there appeared a rather nice middle-aged lady.

The press are often criticised for getting it wrong. Because I had a brother, Noel, who was for many years a foreign correspondent, I suppose I have perhaps more understanding of the problems than some others. The deadline to which they have to work sometimes makes it impossible to check, although there are no doubt some cynics who adhere to the old adage: 'if you've got a good story, don't check it'. But sometimes the facts are simply not there to be established. I mention just one example which over the years has given rise to much speculation.

It was in January 1974 that, to conserve our coal stocks, industry was restricted to a three-day working week. As part of its counter-inflation policy, the Government had laid down statutory criteria for restraining pay increases, but the miners contended that they were a special case. The policy of the Government was clear. It was to stand firm because we had good reason to believe that if we were to agree to treat the miners as a special case, other groups of workers would demand that they, too, deserved special treatment.

On 9 January I was taking the chair at a regular meeting of the National Economic Development Council. In the midst of a general discussion, without any prior indication, Sidney Greene on behalf of the TUC said that if the miners were treated as a special case other unions would not use that as an argument in their own nego-tiations. I knew that the TUC had made it clear, on many other occasions, that while they could use their good offices they simply did not have the authority to compel individual unions to abide by their advice. Therefore the offer to assist was not one which the TUC could deliver.

There was another factor which made me suspicious. If this was truly a genuine offer, and not merely a tactic to wrong-foot the Government, why had the TUC not given us prior warning of the offer so that I would have been in a position to give a considered response? Instead of which, they were asking for an immediate reply. I knew that if without further consultation with other minis-ters I were to agree to consider the proposal, the mere fact that I had agreed to consider it would, without doubt, be interpreted as a major change of stance and indeed as the beginning of the slippery slope. Therefore I turned down the proposal but made it clear to my ministerial colleagues that I would be quite content if, after proper consideration, they wished to pursue it.

Ever since it has been assumed that I contacted nobody outside the meeting. *The Times* reported that I acted without reference to the Prime Minister. Others have made the same point. The truth is that because I did not completely trust the NEDC staff, I decided not to use the NEDC switchboard. I therefore spoke to No. 10 on an outside line.

One other observation. I do not believe that the problem would have arisen if Victor Feather had still been General Secretary of the

TUC. If the offer had been genuine, he would most certainly have given me advance warning. I had developed a close and trusting relationship with him. He was a great patriot. I remember on one occasion when, after an abortive meeting, we had to face a press conference together. At that particular time there was a danger of a run on the pound. I told Victor, in confidence, about the seriousness of the situation and asked him not to rock the boat too much. We met the press and I put the best gloss I could on the failed meeting. It was then open to Victor to give his version. Instead of lambasting the Government, he simply said 'I agree with the Chancellor' and refused to be drawn further.

If a major news item appears which is untrue, it is normally essential to scotch it immediately before it is picked up by the rest of the media. I say 'normally' because in the case of speculative stories about changes in taxation the wisest course is generally to refuse to affirm or deny them. But even here there has to be the occasional exception. One such striking example occurred in December 1971. I was in Rome attending a meeting of the Group of Ten Finance Ministers. Also in Rome to report on the meeting were two of the most senior and reputable economic editors – Sam Brittan of the *Financial Times* and Peter Jay of *The Times*. They joined a few senior Treasury officials and myself at a small luncheon hosted by the Ambassador. It was an informal and agreeable occasion and after lunch we went our separate ways.

It was not surprising that Sam Brittan and Peter Jay should have come to report on the Rome meeting, for the purpose of the meeting was nothing less than to attempt to hammer out a new parity structure and, in furtherance of this, part of the meeting was in closed session, restricted only to Finance Ministers and Central Bank Governors. The one thing the meeting was definitely not concerned with was United Kingdom taxation. Imagine, therefore, my astonishment when, on the morning following the lunch and the first day's meeting, the front pages of both *The Times* and the *Financial Times* carried a report, datelined 'Rome', that the Treasury was considering cutting Purchase Tax. Remember that this was December, and the reports, if they had been allowed to stand even as speculation, would have had a disastrous effect on pre-Christmas retail sales. Who would buy anything now with the prospect of the price shortly to be reduced?

The facts were that no one in the Treasury had put such a

ABOVE The author at Gibraltar with PRU Spitfire. BELOW From a reconnaissance photograph by the author of enemy-occupied Channel port.

ABOVE Mont-St-Michel. BELOW The arrival of the Russians to liberate the anthor's POW camp.

ABOVE Campaigning in Doncaster. BELOW With Harold Macmillan

On **THURSDAY, 28th October**, the House will meet at 2.30 p.m.

Conclusion of the debate on the United Kingdom and the European
                                             Economic Communities

A MOST IMPORTANT DIVISION WILL TAKE PLACE AT 10.00 P.M. PRECISELY.

THERE WILL BE A FREE VOTE.

Thereafter, the House will Prorogue.   The new Session will be opened
on TUESDAY, 2ND NOVEMBER.

                                    FRANCIS   PYM

21.10.71

A free vote or a three-line whip? (See p.78.)

ON THURSDAY, 28th October, the House will meet at 2.30 p.m.

            DEBATE ON THE UNITED KINGDOM AND THE EUROPEAN COMMUNITIES (final day)
            Speakers: (Mr. Harold Wilson will open for the Opposition)
                      (Mr. R. Maudling will open for the Government)
                      (Mr. J. Callaghan will wind-up for the Opposition)
                      (Mr. E. Heath will wind-up for the Government)

A VITAL DIVISION WILL TAKE PLACE AND YOUR ATTENDANCE AT 9.30 P.M. IS ABSOLUTELY ESSENTIA

NOTE: Suspension of the Rule - Members may like to know that on Monday, Tuesday and
      Wednesday, suspension will depend on the number of Members who have indicated
      to Mr. Speaker their intention to take part.

ON FRIDAY, 29th October, the House will meet at 11 a.m.

                    PROROGATION WILL TAKE PLACE

                                    BOB MELLISH

ON TUESDAY, 2nd November, Her Majesty The Queen will open the New Session of Parliament.

ABOVE, LEFT Outside No.11. RIGHT Ted Heath, Jean Barber and the author at the Party Conference, 1969. BELOW The office rearranged by an IRA bomb.

ABOVE With Mrs Gandhi. BELOW With President Marcos; Jean talking to Imelda Marcos.

ABOVE, LEFT With Emir Kano in West Africa. RIGHT With Margaret Thatcher. BELOW With Malcolm Fraser, ex-Prime Minister of Australia, and Allan Boesak in a South African township.

ABOVE, LEFT With Winnie Mandela, outside not-quite-Thatchers restaurant. RIGHT The author and his second wife Rosemary with John Major at a presentation. BELOW With Nelson Mandela in South Africa.

proposition to me and the idea had never even crossed my mind. Yet these two experienced correspondents had clearly got the story from somewhere. The problem was, as I have said, that normally you never commented on speculative stories about tax changes for the obvious reason that if you denied one rumour you would be expected to comment on others which, if not denied, would be assumed to have some substance. But to say nothing at that time of the year when the speculation had appeared as front page-news in two of the most responsible newspapers would not do. Furthermore, I came to the conclusion that it would not be enough in this case simply to issue a formal denial by a Treasury spokesman. I therefore flew back to London at lunchtime and worked on the aircraft on a statement to be made to the House of Commons that afternoon at 3.30 p.m. In answer to a question from Roy Jenkins, I replied as follows:

> My answer to the other points which the Right Hon Gentleman raised is that, as he knows, successive Chancellors of the Exchequer have always taken the view that speculative stories, however absurd, should be neither affirmed nor denied because to do so inevitably provokes further kite-flying and speculation. I am sure that this attitude is, in general, the right one.
>
> The House will therefore understand why I took no notice of the speculative story which appeared in Monday's *Daily Mail*, but as the inference drawn from later stories in *The Times* and the *Financial Times* was that there was some disclosure of intentions in connection with, or in the course of, international meetings, the circumstances are different, and I therefore thought it right, at the first opportunity after my return this morning, that I should tell the House that such stories were wholly without foundation.
>
> In particular, as the stories which were datelined 'Rome' referred to cuts in purchase tax and the use of the regulator, I would only add that there was no discussion or, indeed, mention of these matters, either formally or informally, and, what is more, they are not being considered.

At that point the story was effectively dead, but there still remained the suspicion in some quarters that, precisely because the story was datelined 'Rome', someone in that small Treasury delegation, led by myself, had said something to spark the report.

Then, while I was still on my feet at the Despatch Box, to every-body's surprise, my PPS arrived on the second bench and thrust a piece of paper into my hand. The *Hansard* report completes the story:

> I have just received authority to inform the House – and Hon Members will realise that I returned from Rome only at lunchtime today – that Mr Sam Brittan has this morning sent a message to the Treasury saying that, in view of the suggestions that are being made, he wishes to make it clear that the stories that Mr Peter Jay and he wrote about reflation were not based in any way on anything that had been said by any member of the United Kingdom delegation to the Group of Ten.

Not every journalist would have volunteered such a statement.

In former times, for the Prime Minister to give a full-length TV interview was something of an occasion, and, because of this, the BBC and ITV companies vied with one another for the opportunity. In those circumstances the Prime Minister's Office could lay down reasonable conditions for the interview. I remember one occasion where the programme had been trailed as a major live TV inter-view with the Prime Minister, Harold Macmillan. He and the inter-viewer were sitting in their appointed chairs in the studio engaged in the usual lighthearted pre-programme chat. There were about four or five minutes to go before the programme was due on air. Calmly, Harold Macmillan rose from his chair and said, 'I'm sure the public will understand if we call it off.' Pandemonium broke out.

What had happened was this. It had previously been agreed that one particularly sensitive overseas topic would be excluded from the discussion. Despite this, the interviewer, with only a few minutes to go, casually said that he would naturally have to ask about the topic, but he would quite understand if the Prime Minister chose not to reply. Harold called me over and I confirmed that it had been clearly agreed that the topic would not be men-tioned. The interviewer said something about 'professional in-tegrity' and it was then that Harold slowly rose from his chair. Needless to say, the interview then proceeded as originally agreed. I wondered how many other politicians would have had the nerve to call the interviewer's bluff in such a dramatic way.

There was one extraordinary episode which involved my family, but about which I knew absolutely nothing until many years after I had retired from political life.

A few miles from our home in Yorkshire there lived the architect John Poulson, who was eventually sent to prison for corruption. Before there was any suspicion of his wrongdoing, I had met him socially on a number of occasions. His wife, a charming lady, was the Chairman of the Yorkshire Area Conservative Ladies Committee and they had two adopted daughters who were good friends of our girls. The four girls decided to have a joint children's party, the cost to be shared between the two families.

As the Poulson saga developed he was the subject of bankruptcy proceedings which were held in public, and then on 22 July 1973 he was arrested. The Director of Public Prosecutions and the police had recommended to the Attorney General, Sir Peter Rawlinson, that criminal proceedings should be instituted immediately, and the Attorney had given his consent. One consequence of the start of criminal proceedings was to put a stop forthwith to the bankruptcy proceedings. All this was public knowledge and was of no particular concern to me. It was not until many years later, when Peter published his memoirs, *A Price Too High,* that I learned how I became involved. I cannot do better (with his kind permission) than to quote this extract from those memoirs:

> On the day of the arrests of Poulson and Pottinger I had asked to come and see me Muir Hunter QC, who had been cross-examining the architect in his bankruptcy proceedings. Because the start of criminal proceedings would halt these hearings, I thought that it was only right to warn Muir Hunter of the arrests which were at that moment taking place.
>
> He listened to what I told him, thanked me and said, 'Well, that has stopped the next stage of my cross-examination, which would have been interesting. I was just coming to a matter concerning the Chancellor of the Exchequer, Anthony Barber.' I froze. So my authorisation the evening before of the arrests had effectively stopped the publicising of the name of a second minister in the saga of the bankruptcy which the press was so avidly reporting! 'It was quite an innocent connection,' went on Muir Hunter. 'The children were friends and the Poulsons and the Barbers had shared between them the costs of a party which the children had held. I was going to

probe how Poulson's share of the costs were entered into his accounts.'

For a moment even the unfairness to Anthony Barber of dragging his name into the scandal because of a children's party escaped me. I could only think what use the press might make of this spectacular development. Obviously no one would believe that the Attorney General had not timed the arrests to stop the name of yet another colleague being brought into the Poulson affair. No wonder the Attorney General wanted to prosecute and to hold a public enquiry! I could already hear ringing in my ears the rumble of outraged editorial prose.

For most of my time at the Treasury I got a reasonably good press, less so towards the end, when it became necessary to introduce some very unpopular and draconian measures to deal with the situation arising from the combination of the fourfold increase in oil prices and the miners' strike. What most people now recall is the depressing dénouement of that period 1970–74: the three-day week, the power cuts, the exceptional violence on the picket lines and the sense that the NUM was getting the upper hand. Just as in 1970, when I was convinced that we were going to win the election, so in 1974 I knew that we were on the way to defeat.

After I retired, I had several not unattractive offers to write my side of the story and I have sometimes wondered whether I might have left a somewhat better understanding of the whole period if I had written a lengthy, detailed and well-researched exposition of the way things developed over those four years. Whether or not I would have been wise to do so, I decided against it, largely because I had myself found such tomes of self-justification somewhat tedious.

Maybe Rab Butler had the answer. He once said that all Chancellors make the same mistake. They stay at the Treasury for one year too long.

20

A New Career

When, at the age of fifty-four, I retired from political life, friends in the Commons were very surprised. After all, I represented a safe Conservative seat where I had excellent relations with the local party, I had enjoyed a fascinating series of political offices, and I still had my wits about me.

There were a number of reasons. I had seen too many politicians soldiering on for too long: 'What are we going to do with old so-and-so?' the Prime Minister would ask the Chief Whip. Then again there was the attraction of being out of the public eye: 'Why did you resist an amendment to Clause 11 of the Finance Bill?' asked a chartered accountant while I was swimming out of my depth at St Tropez. I had also had enough of invariably putting my family second to the job. Most of all, however, I wanted to start one more entirely new full-time career and I had concluded that, once past fifty-five, the right opportunity would be unlikely to present itself for someone who had spent the previous twenty-three years in the House of Commons.

What was not known at that time was that I had decided two years earlier that I would retire from politics at the end of that Parliament. The only person in whom I confided was the Prime Minister, and I told him that, if he wished it, I would be happy to stay as Chancellor until the General Election. The reason for secrecy was obvious. If it had been known that I had decided to go, I would no longer have commanded any authority as Chancellor.

My constituency gave me a great farewell party and, unbeknown to me, my constituency Treasurer, a resourceful man called Geoffrey Lee, had invited Harold Macmillan. Ted Heath had also accepted but then, shortly before the due date, he lost the Leadership election to Margaret Thatcher and was planning a holiday abroad with friends. At this point my Treasurer telephoned Harold and told him that Ted would not now be coming to the party and added 'So you will now be the principal speaker.' Harold Macmillan replied, 'My dear man, I always intended to be!'

Having been Chancellor, it was not surprising that I received a number of financially attractive business offers. But I wanted something different. Put another way, the last thing I wanted was a clutch of non-executive directorships where I would turn up for periodic board meetings but where, in the nature of things, I could never be fully involved with the business.

Six months after leaving the Treasury, I became Chairman of the Standard Chartered Bank. Before I accepted I made two stipulations. First, I would not be involved with any lobbying of my old political colleagues and, second, while I had neither the wish nor the competence to pretend to take charge of the detailed day-to-day affairs of the bank, I was to be a full-time Chairman with executive powers. In fact during my thirteen years as Chairman I accepted only one directorship outside the Standard Chartered Group and that was as a Government Director of BP.

There are two people who can make a major contribution to the efficient and relatively carefree life of a busy chairman – his private secretary and his chauffeur. I changed both. To the dismay of the Bank's personnel department, I brought back to London the private secretary to the Chief Manager in Hong Kong. Enid Alce was used to working Hong Kong hours and she soon took charge of my life. One other change. I inherited the Chairman's apartment in Park Lane. It was both comfortable and attractive with a verandah overlooking the Park, but I decided against it. After my years in 11 Downing Street, I had been looking forward to returning to my own home. And I should not forget the customary bank chairman's Rolls-Royce. I suppose it was my politician's sensitivity, but a Rolls-Royce seemed to me to be slightly vulgar and was accordingly replaced by a Bentley. Before I retired from the bank I went one stage further and was provided with a Bristol – my idea of a real car.

Many years had passed since a reporter from the local newspaper asked my young daughter what it was like to have a father who was an MP. She innocently replied: 'I don't know why my Daddy doesn't get a proper job.' Well, now I had.

To start an entirely new career at the age of fifty-four is exciting enough in itself but to be invited to head an organisation like Standard Chartered was doubly exciting. Here was a group which was little known by the general public in this country, because it had only a handful of branches in the UK. Yet it employed some 50,000 people around the world, and had over 2,000 offices in more than 70 countries. Its origins went back to the middle of the last century. The two principal components of the group were the Chartered Bank and the Standard Bank. They had merged in 1970. Each of them had a fascinating earlier history.

When the Chartered Bank petitioned for its Royal Charter in 1852, its full title was The Chartered Bank of India, Australia and China. The founder of the bank was one James Wilson, the son of a prosperous Quaker family. He was a man of many parts and among his other achievements he founded *The Economist* in 1843 and in the early years wrote much of the contents himself. Later he was to enter Parliament and become Financial Secretary. The bank was established, so the prospectus stated, to extend the 'legitimate facilities of banking to the vast and rapidly expanding trade between the Australian Colonies, British India, China and other parts of the Eastern Archipelago'.

The Standard Bank, established in 1862, was the oldest bank in Africa south of the Sahara. Its history began before the days of the first stage-coach in the South when the native runner, with his cleft stick for messages, was the only recognised means of communication in much of the continent. The first office to be established in South Africa was at Port Elizabeth, and already within two years of the formation of the bank fifteen more offices had been opened. The Standard Bank went from strength to strength, overcoming all manner of difficulties. It expanded far and wide. I mention just one recorded episode. When the Bank opened for business in Salisbury, Rhodesia (now Harare, Zimbabwe) the only available sleeping accommodation for the new manager to pass his first few nights was 'a newly erected fowl-house'.

The nature of Standard Chartered Bank and its business, and the fact that it had a worldwide presence in both the most sophisticated and the least developed countries, meant that it attracted a more adventurous type of employee than one would normally find in a British domestic bank. He would know when he joined that he might equally well find himself in Zurich or in some remote branch in the Far East or Africa but, having said that, the expatriates were well cared for. The day was long gone since the new manager in Salisbury slept in a fowl-house. There were generous education allowances and, however remote the posting, arrangements were made for children at boarding school to return regularly to their parents.

In many places the manager and his wife were regarded as persons of considerable status and were expected to involve themselves in the life of the local community. Gone were the days when the wife's principal function was to 'pay, pack and follow'. The history of Standard Chartered is a history of change. There was almost always a political upheaval in one of the countries where we operated. Whether in Mozambique or Iran, Ghana or the Seychelles, a coup (bloodless or otherwise) was just one more situation where the Standard Chartered banker had to use his initiative and ingenuity. While we were opening up in new areas, in others we had to come to terms with nationalisation or liquidation. Such was the case in South Vietnam, Burma, Cambodia, Libya, Iraq, Tanzania and Angola.

We were the oldest bank in Hong Kong and, because of this, we originally provided the permanent Chairman of the Exchange Banks Association which, *inter alia*, controlled the exchange rates. Over the years, the Chief Manager in Hong Kong had to cope with a variety of problems, including riots and the Cultural Revolution when eight branches were destroyed.

Those who possessed the qualities to rise to senior management were men of many parts. And the best of their wives were a very special breed. Far from home, they not only had to deal with the particular problems which distance posed for their own families, but were expected to minister to the needs of the younger and less experienced wives who might, perhaps, be worried about one of their own children at boarding school many thousands of miles away. And on top of all this, as I have said, they were expected to take an active interest in the affairs of the local community. The bank owes much to these wives but, of course, there was never any question of paying them!

Businessmen travelling overseas are sometimes criticised for taking their wives. Of course, like any other aspects of foreign travel, it is open to abuse, but I have to say that, in the case of my own travels, the contribution which Jean made was invaluable. There was no point in her accompanying me on short visits to attend overseas board meetings, but a three-week tour to distant parts of the world is a different matter. In the first place, she would learn much from the wives of members of the staff which would otherwise never have been known to the Chairman. Then there was the social side, be it with customers, staff or members of the overseas Government. There was the occasion when the Governor of the Central Bank in Sierra Leone invited my wife and me to dinner. Jean tipped me off that he was intending to make a speech. I had a word with the Governor's wife and the upshot was that I made my shortest speech ever. I asked the Governor's wife how to say in the local patois: 'Thank you for an excellent dinner. I look forward to seeing you again.' It came out like this: 'Tankee for de good chop. I tink I go come back.' At the same dinner I was told that the Minister of Finance was known as 'De man mit de money bags'.

Because of the worldwide spread of the bank's operations, the position of the Chairman involved much travel. These overseas visits fell broadly into two categories. There were those where the purpose was to sort out some problem with the authorities. Sometimes the visit could just as well have been made by a senior member of management but, in some of the developing countries where they were particularly sensitive to rank, the Minister of Finance, for instance, might expect to be visited by the Chairman himself.

Then there was the other category of visits where the primary object was to show the flag. In many of the developing countries where we operated we were virtually part of the establishment and close relations with the Government and the banking authorities were crucial. In the poorer countries the bank often had a major role to play in developing the local economy. Furthermore, in those countries where we had maintained a presence over a long period, our customers knew that, even though the bank might find the general economic climate unfavourable for a few years, provided the future was not wholly bleak, we would not pull out. We were there for the long term and we took the view that if we had enjoyed the prosperous years then we had an obligation to see them through the difficult years.

21

People and Places

I suppose it was inevitable that, after my years in politics, I should already know many of the notables that I was now to meet again, this time on behalf of the bank. I found it almost embarrassing that, time and again, when the bank had arranged for me to call on some Head of State or Prime Minister of a country where we operated, I would reply in no sense boastfully that we had met several times before. But with the passage of time what remains uppermost in my mind, in most instances, is some probably quite inconsequential aspect or incident.

Arrangements had been made for me to see Mrs Gandhi at her home, and I naturally thought that she would want to say something about the economic and social problems of India. Not a bit of it. Her overriding concern was with a mildly critical leader which had appeared in the London *Times* a few days earlier. What she wanted was to be thought well of by her English friends, and I realised then what an important influence her English education must have been. There were many men and women in high places around the world whose friendship for Britain stemmed from their student days at a British university. I remember reflecting, as I left Mrs Gandhi's house, that the British Government was probably wrong to cut back the financial assistance which had previously been available to foreign students. Lord Carrington as Foreign Secretary fought to retain it. As Chancellor my purpose was to contain the rising public expenditure. Maybe this was one case where I should have gracefully given way.

It was on an earlier visit to India that I found myself sitting next to the Chief of the General Staff. The time he had spent at Sandhurst had left an indelible mark on his manners and his mannerisms. It was almost as though a caricature had come to life. I mentioned to him that earlier that day I had been talking with the Indian Minister of Health about the preferred means of birth control which was the 'loop', and I asked him whether the Indian Army was doing anything to encourage birth control. 'Certainly,' he replied, 'I have instructed that notices should be prominently displayed in all barracks with the simple message "Loop before you leap!"'

If charm is the word which sums up my recollection of Mrs Gandhi, arrogance is the word which best describes the Shah. Peter Walker, who was then Secretary of State for Trade and Industry, had got to know the Shah well and had successfully negotiated some very advantageous arrangements, the essence of which involved bartering Iranian oil for British exports. Peter was due to make a further visit and, somewhat surprisingly, the Shah sent a message asking that the Chancellor of the Exchequer should also travel to see him about some of the financial aspects. I could see that here was an opportunity to persuade the Shah to deposit more of his oil revenues in London. I had expected the meeting to take place at the Shah's palace in Teheran, but was told that he and his senior ministers would all be at his chalet in St Moritz.

One or two of the popular newspapers were very critical of the idea of the Chancellor of the Exchequer going 'cap in hand' to the Shah. Because of this, I was determined that the press should have no opportunity to portray the visit as a frolic. Declining the invitation for my wife to accompany me, I arrived in St Mortiz in a formal, dark city suit, only to find myself photographed with the Shah's entourage all dressed in *après-ski* wear. I looked quite ridiculous.

After the lunch, and when the business meetings were concluded, the Shah ordered his ministers to leave. There were just the two of us. To my astonishment he then proceeded to lecture me about deteriorating standards in Britain. This man, who controlled Savak, one of the nastiest and most cruel secret services in the modern world, had the effrontery to talk to me about decadence in Britain. I argued courteously but, in view of the purpose of the visit, I was in no position to speak my mind as forcefully as I would have wished. At least as far as the ministerial visit was concerned, an excellent deal was secured for the United Kingdom and both Peter and I arrived home laden with caviar!

Several years later, after I had retired from the Commons, I became a director of the Irano-British Bank, the Chairman of which had been the Shah's Trade Minister. My earlier opinion of the

Shah was confirmed and in due course he fell. 'Pride goeth before destruction, and an haughty spirit before a fall.'

Despite all the justified criticism of President Marcos I found him an agreeable man to talk to. Jean was with me and we had to wait about twenty minutes before Marcos arrived. During that time we were looked after by his wife, Imelda. I could see that she had been a great beauty in her younger days, and there was no evidence of her reputed forceful character. Not satisfied with being the First Lady of the Philippines she was also Mayor of Manila. I asked her how that came about. 'I was drafted,' she replied.

The occasion for my visit to the Philippines was to attend the IMF/World Bank meeting which was being held in Manila. That meeting provided a classic example of how a government, at great expense, can create entirely the wrong impression. An enormous hall had been built specially for the meeting. All the arrangements were lavish in the extreme. So there we were, many of us driving each morning through some of the worst of the Manila slums on our way to the meeting where we solemnly listened to speeches about Third World poverty.

In fairness to Marcos, I suppose that it should be remembered that the IMF/World Bank meeting is held outside Washington only once in every three years, and it follows that this is the one and only opportunity the country will ever have to act as host to all the World's Finance Ministers and Central Bank Governors, as well as representatives from most of the world's commercial banks. In those countries where power and wealth are synonymous, I suppose it is natural that they should want to push the boat out.

On the morning after I had seen Marcos, a banking colleague told me that it had been reported on the radio that I had told Marcos that Standard Chartered was ready to make some major facility available to the Philippines. It was wholly untrue.

On my first visit to Bangkok the bank had arranged for me to call on the King of Thailand. As we waited in the anteroom at the palace where I was to have the audience, I could just see through the open door a number of Thais taking their leave. They appeared to be moving backwards on their hands and knees until they were out of the room. I quickly took some advice from the Palace dignitary who was accompanying me and was assured that no such obeisance was necessary in my case. But witnessing such servility I wondered what sort of man I was going to meet.

If I had thought that I was going to meet a playboy king, I could not have been more wrong. Despite his opulent surroundings, it soon became clear that here was a man with a mission. He spent almost all his time telling me of the practical ways in which he personally was involved in improving the lot of the poor. He talked eagerly, and with obvious detailed technical knowledge, of programmes such as the sinking of wells. I was no longer surprised that he was such a revered figure.

Lee Kuan Yew and Mugabe are two men who would be extremely surprised to be bracketed together. The one attribute they have in common is that they are both realists. Everyone knows the story of Singapore. With no natural resources, Singapore owes its remarkable success to the resolute leadership of one man. There are some in the West who would criticise him for having dealt somewhat harshly with those who opposed him, but one thing I have learnt during my travels is that rights and customs which we hold dear in Britain are often quite inappropriate elsewhere.

Standard Chartered has a major presence in Singapore and, while I was Chairman, we opened a new 42-storey Head Office there. But I had called to see Lee Kuan Yew from time to time before that. On one such occasion, Margaret Thatcher had just been elected Leader of the Conservative Party, but was not yet Prime Minister. Harry Lee said something to the effect: 'She is obviously very able, but I can't see a woman as Prime Minister of Britain.' 'What about Golda Meier?' I replied. 'That's different . . .,' he retorted. I cannot recall his concluding words!

Mugabe was another realist. He knew that I was on the Board of the Standard Bank of South Africa, then a subsidiary of Standard Chartered, but his concern was simply that the bank in Zimbabwe with some forty offices should operate efficiently in the interests of Zimbabwe. Throughout the period of UDI the bank in London had no control over the operations in Zimbabwe. As soon as possible after independence I paid my first visit. What surprised me was not just the efficiency of the staff, but the excellent state of the premises despite the many years of sanctions. I naturally paid a courtesy call on the new first President, the Reverend Canaan Banana. It will be remembered that, during the transitional period to independence, Christopher Soames had been installed for a short period as Governor and had been living in Government House. The Reverend Canaan Banana, who was a teetotaller, offered me a

drink and I asked for a whisky. A manservant duly arrived with a
large tumbler, almost half full of whisky. Clearly Christopher had
left his mark. Incidentally, I had heard that the latest cocktail to
be served in Meikles Hotel was a 'Cane and Banana', but I was
strongly advised not to request one at Government House.

With the bank's extensive network of offices around the world, I
found myself travelling overseas for two to three months every year
– from Peking to New York, from Sarawak to Nigeria. It was
in Northern Nigeria that our local manager noticed that my six-
months' cholera inoculation was out of date, and I was flying back
to London that evening. I explained that this would be no problem
at the London end and that surely, as I was leaving their country,
the Nigerians would not be concerned. The manager replied that I
did not understand the workings of the Nigerian bureaucracy. I
must admit that, probably unfairly, I did not relish the thought of
that needle being administered in that part of the world. But I need
not have worried. Our managers overseas were always resourceful
and he had the answer. 'I can easily arrange for your medical card
to be stamped without your having to attend.' Somewhat hesitat-
ingly I acquiesced and, when the card was returned, I commented
that, having been Minister of Health, I felt a twinge of guilt in
having the official stamp on my card with no inoculation having
been administered. 'But it has,' replied the manager, 'my man had
the jab.'

We had some unusual customers. I remember during my first
visit to the Gulf calling at a small branch at an oasis called Al Ain,
on the edge of the desert. The young manager had arranged for me
to visit his most important customer – Sheikh Shakhbut. So off we
went into the desert to meet him. Sheikh Shakhbut had been the
Ruler of Abu Dhabi before he was overthrown and banished to
the desert. He was generously provided for financially by the new
Ruler, who paid him a regular stipend. The story went that he
used to bank with one of our competitors until he entered that
bank one day, without notice, and asked to see his accumulated
funds. Of course the branch did not have enough cash available at
that particular moment. Sheikh Shakhbut, not being cognisant of
the niceties of banking, immediately closed his account and moved
to Standard Chartered. Every month thereafter the local manager
travelled into the desert with a case full of cash. Where the accumulated cash was stored we never learned.

One thing puzzled me. There we were in the desert in circumstances which seemed just about as far removed from London as it was possible to be, yet the Sheikh's whole topic of conversation was the current British political scene. How come that he was so well informed? The answer was that he was an avid listener to the BBC Overseas Service. I suppose that if you were banished to the desert that was as good a way as any of spending your time.

That was during my first visit to the Gulf as Chairman of the bank. Together with John Peyton, I had first travelled round the Middle East some forty years ago. Then it was all very different. Although the Ruler of Kuwait was already fabulously rich, the small Sultanate of Oman had not yet discovered oil. We landed on a grass strip outside Muscat, and we went first to call on the Shell representative who was in charge of the search for oil. All I recall of that meeting is that, to my surprise, when I entered his room there was the voice of Eartha Kitt coming from an old gramophone.

We next went to call on the Sultan. We were escorted up a long stone staircase flanked by what looked to me suspiciously like Nubian slaves, and then entered a reception room with an outlook on to a most beautiful bay. The Sultan had been educated in India and spoke good English. By way of making conversation I said, 'I expect Your Highness will be very pleased if they find oil', to which he replied, 'Yes, but I expect that we shall have to have Coca Cola as well'.

My years with the bank were more than illuminating. Unlike overseas travel as the Chancellor, which generally consisted of a short visit, staying with the Ambassador, and returning to London as soon as the business was completed, I got now a much deeper insight into the various countries where we had branches or subsidiaries.

I suppose that the two most exhilarating areas which I used to visit were California, where we acquired Union Bank, and Hong Kong, where we had a network of more than a hundred branches. Hong Kong is a very different place now but, when I joined the bank, there were more than twenty years to go before the handover to China. Whether it was in Los Angeles or in Hong Kong, I never found the materialism of these thrusting enterprising people offensive. There was one of our Los Angeles directors, a self-made multimillionaire, who named his yacht the *Dry Martini* and the dinghy the *Twist of Lemon*. I enjoyed every minute of it.

I remember once taking the chair in New Orleans for Milton Friedman. He was expounding the virtues of the free market economy and he cited Hong Kong as the supreme example. What he omitted to add was that the reason for Hong Kong's unique achievement was twofold – the absence of any serious democratic control and the presence of an efficient administration, a combination it would be difficult to find elsewhere.

In Hong Kong they always did things on the grand scale. The bank held a dinner every year for the members of staff. One year I was in the colony to join them. Typical of Hong Kong, all 3,000 staff were accommodated in a single restaurant and each one of the fourteen courses of the Chinese dinner were served simultaneously.

So much for the glamorous places. There were also Beirut, Uganda and Bangladesh, to mention but three, where one saw a different side.

Chittagong is the southernmost port of Bangladesh – a desperately poor country – and I was told that no Chairman of the Bank had ever visited the Chittagong branch. So down I went to receive a welcome I will never forget. Was this what it was like in the days of the Raj? I was placed on a sort of dais and the senior clerk proceeded to read out an Address of Welcome on behalf of the staff. Modesty forbids my quoting it in full, but here is an extract.

May your Lordship condescend to warm us with a radiating grace and noble patience:

We, the members of the staff of The Chartered Bank, Chittagong Branch congratulate ourselves on the privilege granted to us for welcoming an august personage of your Lordship's eminence in our midst on your visit to this far-flung branch of your great organisation.

We recall with wonder and admiration your resourcefulness during the myriad vicissitudes of the Second World War, which was waged to save humanity from the Nazi and Fascist domination. Like the Ulysses of old, your Lordship beguiled the vigilance of the Nazi prison-guards by organising an escape committee.

We are thankful that a man of your Lordship's greatness has been pleased to take up the stewardship of the vast organisation, Standard Chartered Bank Limited.

We fervently pray to God and seek the good office of your

Lordship so that we may be enabled to efficiently and faith-
fully perform the task assigned to us.

May God grant you a long and happy lease of life for the
vital interest of this vast organisation which may expand and
prosper under your Lordship's dynamic personality.

May your Lordship please to remember us all – the humble
members of your great organisation.

22

Seeing for Myself

Wherever I travelled the local bank made staff available to me and because of this I had no need to take a personal assistant or secretary. On only one occasion did I make an exception and that was when I attended the IMF/World Bank meeting in Manila. I wanted someone at once agreeable and reliable to organise a variety of meetings and social functions and I picked a youngish man who had been with the bank for some years and who I thought would fill the bill. His name was John Major.

I suppose that, because I had been Chairman of the party, from time to time young men sought my advice as to whether they should embark on a political career. In the case of a man with a good job and a family to support my advice was almost invariably the same. I cautioned them against it, for all too often a budding politician would get into the House holding a marginal seat which he was bound to lose in due course. Then he would be out, still with a family to support but with no seat and no job. I mention this because, exceptionally in the case of John Major, I positively encouraged him to go ahead.

He seemed to me to have so many of the qualities to make a successful political career. I had absolutely no doubt, even in those early days, that if he could find a constituency to accept him, he would go far and, certainly if he were fortunate enough to get a safe seat, he would in due course join the Cabinet. I have to admit that I did not visualise him going quite so far so quickly.

I have already mentioned my attendance at the Annual Meetings of the IMF/World Bank in my capacity as Chancellor. Now I was at the Manila meeting as a commercial banker and I decided that instead of hosting just another reception I would organise something a little more ambitious. And so a group of Filipino dancers come to perform on the lawn of our manager's house. The evening was an outstanding success and those staid middle-aged bankers required no encouragement to join in the dancing. Whether or not our future Prime Minister took part I cannot recollect.

On my return to London I put John Major in charge of the bank's public affairs with a view to his returning, in due course, to a banking career proper. In the event, he was selected for Huntingdon – which had the largest Conservative majority in the country. The rest we know.

When the Standard Bank and the Chartered Bank merged to form a group operating in more than seventy countries around the world, they overlapped in only three places – London, New York and Hamburg. So, geographically, it was a perfect merger. Before the merger, when the Conservatives were previously in opposition, I had been on the Court of the Chartered Bank – because it had a Royal Charter, it was controlled by a Court rather than a board of directors. In the early days of the merger there was a certain amount of tension between the two arms of the new group and, because of my previous association with the Chartered side, I deemed it politic to make my first overseas visit to the Standard offices in Africa. And so I set off for a three-week tour of West Africa – to The Gambia, Sierra Leone, Ghana and, finally, Nigeria.

The Gambia is a tiny country and we had only two branches there, one in the capital, Banjul, and the other at Basse, a couple of days travelling by boat up the Gambia River. Our manager had arranged for me to give a dinner for the local worthies, and the Governor of the Central Bank reciprocated with another dinner in my honour. Within hours I was violently ill with food poisoning. So were most of our guests. Our young manager was full of remorse, until it transpired that there was one individual who was ill who had not been at our function but had been at the dinner hosted by the Governor. So the bank was in the clear, and there was relief all round.

But my own problem remained. I was still laid low and, even if I had been prepared to travel, the nature of my affliction meant that there were obvious practical problems which made it inadvisable. What concerned me was the impression which would be created if on this, my first overseas visit, I had to delay my arrival in the other three West African states where I knew they had laid on very full programmes for the visit of the new Chairman. My own medication which I had brought with me from London, in anticipation of just such an eventuality, had no effect whatsoever.

Once again, I need not have worried. A large African doctor was called in and, with an engaging smile, handed me a bottle which he assured me had never failed. Its effect was miraculous, but my relief gradually turned to increasing concern as I travelled from The Gambia, completed a full programme in Sierra Leone and then on to Ghana with the miracle remedy still 100% effective. I remembered that the President of The Gambia, Sir Dawda Jawara, was a qualified vet and I began to wonder whether by some mistake his surgery had been the source of the miracle cure. Fortunately, by the time I reached Lagos all was well.

People often talk of the great divide between the prosperous North and the impoverished South. But travelling around the world there was another contrast which always remained with me – the contrast between urban poverty and poverty in the countryside. Dacca, Manila, Jakarta – it was these and other city slums which I found most disturbing. I still have a vivid recollection of one afternoon in Bombay, taking afternoon tea in the best hotel, listening to the strains of Viennese music and glancing out of the window to see very small children (and I mean very small) darting dangerously in and out of the traffic holding their hands out in the hope of being given some pittance.

I know that it is illogical, but poverty in the countryside somehow seemed more bearable. There was the little boy scrabbling among the bushes, collecting and eating beetles. He did not look unhealthy and the African manager who was with me – who was not an unkind man – calmly observed that there was a lot of protein in beetles!

Although I occasionally travelled to Australia or Los Angeles for some meeting and stayed only a day or two before returning, I would normally try to arrange a three-week tour of the distant areas. These tours were fascinating but also tiring and I generally planned to take it easy during the weekends. On one such occasion I was invited to spend a weekend in Assam.

I went from the depressing squalor of Calcutta to a valley of exquisite beauty and the peace and quiet of a tea plantation, or tea garden as they are properly known. Arrangements had been made for me to be flown in what must surely have been one of the oldest and most decrepit single-engine aircraft in existence. The pilot was a tiny man who had to sit on two cushions and even then had to crane his neck upwards to see out of the cockpit. If his appearance did not inspire confidence, neither did his casual opening remark that some of the instruments (of which there were few) were not working. By way of encouragement he explained that the weather was perfect and that we would be flying over open country and that there would therefore be no problem about a forced landing. We landed safely at Gauhati and it was not long before we arrived at the tea garden where I was to stay. Set in the Brahmaputra valley against the backdrop of the Himalayas, it was sheer beauty.

The evening was memorable if somewhat incongruous. It was spent at the plantation managers' clubhouse where, after a few beers, we sat down to watch Barbra Streisand in the film *The Way We Were*. Every now and then there was a pause while the Indian projectionist changed the reels and we all had another beer. I found it impossible to follow the story and wondered whether it was the beer. The explanation was soon forthcoming. The projectionist apologised for having got the reels the wrong way round.

23

Mergers and Acquisitions

Soon after I became Chairman, we had to deal with a problem which arose in the United States. We had an important presence in New York and had gradually built up a network of some thirty branches in California. It had been decided that any substantial expansion should take place on the West Coast, but there was a problem. Because the Chase Manhattan Bank had an eleven per cent stake in Standard Chartered, it appeared that we were precluded by the Banking Authorities from expanding in the United States. Indeed, we were being pressed to divest ourselves of the branch network in California.

The solution was for Chase Manhattan to divest itself of its holding in Standard Chartered. It was in connection with this problem that I went to New York to see David Rockefeller, then Chairman of Chase Manhattan. I had met him before from time to time when I was Chancellor, and it was typical of him that he should have laid on a large luncheon to enable me to meet many of the most senior figures in the New York banking scene. The upshot was that Chase Manhattan did agree to divest itself of its shareholding in Standard Chartered, thus opening the way for us to expand in the United States.

In all that followed, Peter Graham, the Managing Director, and I worked in tandem. As Chief Manager in Hong Kong for nearly ten years, he had been responsible for building a network in the colony of more than 100 branches and he was an international banker of wide experience.

Our strategy was to make a major expansion on the West Coast. As I have mentioned, we already had some thirty comparatively small branches, mainly in Northern California, but we knew that we would never be able to achieve a major presence by what was known as *de novo* expansion – establishing a series of new branches. We had to acquire an existing major bank and any acquisition had to be by agreement. We called to see Arthur Burns, the Chairman of the Federal Reserve, whom I knew well from my time at the Treasury. He gave us a warm welcome but made it clear that the Authorities would not look kindly on a contested takeover bid.

It was while we were looking for a major Californian bank to acquire that I became friendly with Tom Wilcox, the Chief Executive of Crocker Bank, one of the largest banks in the State. There was no question of our ever considering taking over a bank the size of Crocker, but one evening Tom Wilcox broached the idea of some link between Standard Chartered and Crocker which would involve a close working relationship to our mutual advantage. There were a number of possibilities, ranging from a loose association to some form of cross-shareholding. I talked the matter over with Peter Graham and, while neither of us saw any future in the proposal, I thought the approach sufficiently important to report it to the Board.

The reason why I recount this episode is that, because Midland Bank had at that time a minority shareholding in Standard Chartered, we had on our Board an executive director of Midland, Malcolm Wilcox. Malcolm would therefore have known that Crocker was interested in a possible link with another bank. Was this a factor in the development of close relations between Crocker and Midland? The fact is that the two Wilcoxes, Tom and Malcolm, did get together. Midland eventually took control until various problems necessitated a very expensive unravelling.

As everyone in the banking world knows, for reasons I need not elaborate, the arrangement proved to be absolutely disastrous for Midland. That once great bank – at one time the biggest bank in the world – found itself saddled with an enormous burden of Crocker's bad and doubtful debts. Had that approach from Crocker to Standard Chartered which I reported to the Board provided the spark of an idea in the mind of Malcolm Wilcox?

In our search for a major bank on the West Coast, we had made up our mind that we would not be interested in anything short of 100% control. It was not that we had any wish to run an American bank on a day-to-day basis, but we wanted to be in a position to exercise complete control to ensure that nothing went seriously wrong.

We first set our sights on the Bank of California, a bank with the then unique franchise to operate in three Western states. We made the appropriate overtures in San Francisco where the bank had its head office, but without success. We then went to Paris to see the largest shareholder, Baron Edmond de Rothschild. He gave us an excellent lunch at his home where we were welcomed with some of his family's outstanding wine. It was a most agreeable occasion, but we returned empty-handed.

Eventually, after much lobbying in Washington and Sacramento and a visit to Governor Jerry Brown, we acquired Union Bank, then the sixth largest bank in California. Its strategy was much more in tune with our style, very business-orientated and particularly strong in Los Angeles and Southern California where our own presence was light. The Chairman was one Harry Volk, who stayed on for some time and with whom we had excellent relations. His wife, Maggie, had been a television actress. Both she and Harry became close personal friends. Together with our own small branch network in the state, Union Bank gave us the presence which we wanted. Because Union Bank was wholly owned subsidiary of Standard Chartered, I joined their Board and was always invigorated by their meetings and my visits around the state. I remember visiting one small drive-in branch where the teller casually mentioned that if a customer turned up with a dog in the car he, the teller, would shoot down a dog biscuit with the cash.

Then there was what appeared to be a somewhat bizarre request from Norman Eckersley, our Chief Manager in San Francisco. Would I use my good offices to arrange for Magna Carta to be exhibited in the bank's premises throughout California? What seemed to me at first to be almost a joke arose out of the United States Bicentenary Celebrations, when, as part of the British contribution, a group of US Senators were invited to London to carry back Magna Carta to Washington on loan for one year to the Library of Congress. Our man in San Francisco had read that there were in fact several originals of Magna Carta, and he went on to say that the West Coast did not see why they should not have one of the originals on show there.

I did a little research and found that there still existed four originals of the Charter of 1215, two of them in the cathedral churches in which they were originally deposited, Lincoln and Salisbury, and the other two in the British Museum. I telephoned an old friend who was a Trustee of the British Museum; he told me that the best of the four surviving originals was the one in Lincoln Cathedral. There was only one thing to do. I got on the phone to the Dean, The Very Revd Hon. Oliver Twistleton-Wykeham-Fiennes, and asked him whether I might call to see him. I did not explain why.

I duly turned up at the Deanery for tea the following Friday afternoon on my way home to Yorkshire and began by asking him if he had heard of Standard Chartered. He replied that he had not. I then explained what I had in mind and mentioned that the bank in California would be happy to make a donation of US $10,000 to any fund connected with the cathedral. To my considerable surprise, the Dean was encouraging. It appeared that the Chapter had already had a similar idea themselves, and within an astonishingly short space of time a plan was agreed. It was necessary to move quickly, for it was already half way through the bicentennial year.

A case, proof against every possible peril, was designed, tested and built. Magna Carta was sealed within two sheets of armoured glass (as it happened by a Mr Carter of the British Museum). A schedule was arranged and the Dean (who turned out to be a descendant of one of the barons of 1215) and his wife were invited to escort the document. Massive security was prepared.

So, on 30 September, thirty seconds ahead of time, a Vulcan bomber of No. 9 Squadron RAF landed at Castle Air Force Base, and Magna Carta, escorted by helicopters, spotter planes and a mass of police, duly arrived at the Chartered Bank of London in San Francisco. It evoked enormous interest throughout California, and the visit of the Dean and his wife was an outstanding success.

I have said that, geographically, the combination of Standard Chartered Bank was a perfect merger. But no commercial organisation can stand still and so, after some years, we realised that the next step for the Group, which was strong overseas but comparatively small in the United Kingdom, was to join up with a bank which was big in the United Kingdom but with a modest presence overseas. The Royal Bank of Scotland was just such a bank.

Peter Graham had known Michael Herries, the Chairman of the Royal Bank, when they were both working in Hong Kong. After lengthy and detailed secret discussions, we announced publicly the decision of the two Boards of Directors to merge the two banks. Before going public, we had settled all the major issues. I was to be

Chairman of the new bank which would have been the third largest
bank in the UK. But it was not to be. What was without doubt in
the best interests of both Standard Chartered and the Royal Bank of
Scotland was vetoed by the Monopolies Commission – and by a
majority of one!

Once it became known that our strategy was to look for a
partner, there was much speculation about the likelihood of other
major banks considering making a takeover bid for us. Eventually,
in 1986, the bid came from Lloyds Bank. In the event, over a period
of some months, we fought them off.

I was personally somewhat unhappy about the outcome. I always felt that there was much to be said for a merger with Lloyds
Bank. They were a very efficient domestic bank in the United
Kingdom where Standard Chartered had little presence and their
overseas presence complemented our own. I had known Sir Jeremy
Morse, their Chairman, from way back when he was in the Bank of
England and I was a Treasury Minister. I would have been quite
content, in the general interest, to serve as his deputy. But the senior
executives at Standard Chartered were adamant and, perhaps more
to the point, so were our non-executive directors and our external
merchant bank advisers. So although I would myself have preferred
at least to talk with Lloyds, I concluded that my duty as Chairman
was to carry out the clear wishes of the Board.

And so the Lloyds bid failed, but it left behind one infuriating
and time-consuming episode. It is a serious criminal offence for any
company to lend money for the purpose of buying that company's
own shares. Some newspapers had begun to hint that we were
doing just that, as part of our defence against Lloyds Bank. Veiled
innuendoes continued, and then, on the morning of 4 February
1987 there appeared a report on the front page of the *Financial
Times* under the headline: 'Standard Chartered Lent to Buyers of Its
Shares'.

Enough was enough. Peter Graham and I knew that we had to
act, and act quickly. We did two things that morning. We issued a
writ for defamation against the *Financial Times* and we walked
over to the Bank of England and requested them to institute a
formal investigation under the Banking Act. The Bank of England
had initiated such investigations on previous occasions, but never
before had they had done so at the request of a bank against which
the allegations were being made. The investigation took many

months to complete, cost over £1 million and, in the event, Standard Chartered was given a completely clean bill of health.

I was myself called to give evidence to the inquiry and was examined for the best part of a day by the Inspectors, one a senior lawyer and the other a senior accountant. There has been much criticism of the inquisitorial type of inquiry and, although I knew when we requested the investigation that we had acted throughout with complete propriety, I nevertheless found the forceful questioning hard to take. A few years previously, knowing that I had absolutely nothing to hide, I would have taken the whole affair in my stride. I wonder now, looking back, whether that was an early symptom of my Parkinson's Disease which was diagnosed some years later.

24
A Chairman's Role

The banks come in for a good deal of criticism these days. If that criticism is levelled at poor personal customer service in the Western world, there may well be some justification for it. The criticism which more often than not is unjustified is the role which the banks play in the economies of the developing countries. It is no exaggeration to say that without the provision of bank finance in the poorer countries it would have been well nigh impossible for them to progress. As I travelled round the Standard Chartered branches, I used to marvel at the great variety of successful ventures which had been made possible by the bank.

Of course there were failures, sometimes due to faulty evaluation by the bank, but more often as the result of poor management by the borrower or of developments which could not have been foreseen. Every loan involves some degree of risk but no banker ever lends money unless he has reason to believe that it will be successfully employed. The problem for the bank manager in some of the remoter parts of Africa or the East is that the accounting methods, or the mere keeping of records, are frequently primitive in the extreme. So he has to rely on other more basic indicators. Is the warehouse or go-down stacked with the customer's finished goods? Or do the manager's periodic visits show that the goods are moving?

It is fashionable in some quarters to castigate the banks for the build-up of Third World debt. It should be remembered that the bank has a duty to those who deposit their funds with it as well as to those who borrow from it. When, in the autumn of 1973, the OPEC countries quadrupled the price of oil, it was obvious that the world would be awash with oil money. I was Chancellor at the time and I cannot recall anyone then criticising the banks for recycling that money and directing it to the developing countries. Furthermore, the general view at that time was that the prospects for growth in the developing world were such that those countries would be able to service the debt. Twenty years ago, when this was happening, the availability of those OPEC funds was thought to be a boon for many of the poorer nations.

I spent thirteen gratifying years as Chairman of Standard Chartered Bank. During those years the bank had grown and changed to meet the increasing competition, not only from other international banks but also from the emerging local banks in the old colonial territories which had now gained their independence. It was always apparent that we would be faced with the prospect of the local banks obtaining a growing share of the local business. In a variety of ways they were often given preferential treatment by the Authorities but, in general, we took the view that this was not unreasonable if they were to get off the ground. Indeed, we went further and would second some of our own staff to the new local bank to help it on its way. We still had one major advantage. Because of our spread of offices around the globe we were often the only bank uniquely placed to service international transactions at both ends with no other bank being involved. The attraction to the customer was that, if anything went wrong, or there was unjustified delay, there could be no doubt about the responsibility.

Although most of our staff were overseas, we built a fine new Head Office on the site of the old Chartered Bank in Bishopsgate where we owned the freehold. The Chairman of our subsidiary and associate companies and our senior executives from around the world all came over to London for a grand opening by the Queen. We twice received the Queen's Award for Export Achievement. This was not only a source of pride for those in the London office but, strange though it may seem, the fact that we had won the Queen's Award was considered a great status symbol by the locals in the countries of the old British Empire.

To the extent that the bank's day-to-day operations changed over the years, that was the province of management. There was one important change which I made gradually during my time as Chairman, and that was to the character and composition of the Main Board. When I became Chairman the non-executive directors were men of distinction and absolute probity, but they tended to put their faith in the Chairman whom they had appointed and in the senior executives whom they justifiably regarded as men of proven ability. This made for Board meetings which were largely

non-contentious. (And they were certainly comfortable and agreeable occasions for the Chairman!) But as the bank expanded and
became more complex, I could see that there was a need for change.
And so, as individual members of the Board retired, I gradually
introduced more business-orientated directors. By the time I retired
there was much more questioning of proposals which came before
the Board. No longer could their smooth passage be taken for
granted. As the Chairman's function became more demanding I
occasionally thought of those earlier Board meetings when there
was never any problem about completing the agenda by 12.50 p.m.
in time to repair for an aperitif before lunch which, in those days,
after a glass or two of wine, ended with port or brandy.

The bank was renowned for its food and wine, and no doubt the
somewhat lavish hospitality emanated from the fact that day in,
day out we entertained visitors from overseas who in all probability, had no further commitments that day. What really influenced
me to change those lunches was the not-infrequent occasions when
I was the guest of leading bankers in New York. A light lunch and
maybe a glass of sherry (as a 'gesture to Lord Barber') but that was
all. I could not help but be impressed. It was not until the evening
that the Martinis began to flow.

When I arrived at Standard Chartered there was no Audit
Committee, no Donations Committee and no Remuneration Committee. It was not long before we established all three and, while on
the mater of remuneration, I might mention two general points
about which I feel particularly strongly. The first concerns the
responsibility of the non-executive director which has grown enor-
mously in recent years. No longer is it enough for him to approve
the appointment of a competent Chief Executive and then let him
get on with the job. It is not only a matter of increased personal
responsibility, but of the time which the non-executive director
now has to spend on the company's business if he is to fulfil his role
adequately. The days are long gone when one joined the Board of a
major company for reasons of prestige, and it follows that no
non-executive who is worth his salt should be expected to serve
without being properly rewarded.

The second aspect of remuneration which concerns me is the
frequent abuse of the three-year rolling contract. All too often the
current contract period is not completed and the executive retires
early with a lump sum payment which, in many cases, is wholly

undeserved. Of course there are cases where a rolling contract may be necessary to attract the right man for a particularly crucial position, but often that is not the case. For the record, I chose to be appointed Chairman year by year with no formal contract and when I retired I received no ex-gratia payment.

Although, as Chairman of Standard Chartered, I worked in the City for thirteen years, I never considered myself part of what I might call the City life. My interest was in the operations of the bank. I am not for one moment saying that the City institutions do not perform an outstanding service in a variety of ways. There is no financial centre anywhere in the world to match the City. I am simply expressing my own personal attitude to the social and more formal side of the City. Perhaps it stemmed from the fact that, over the years, I had had my fill of such occasions. Each year as Chancellor I was the principal speaker at the dinner in the Mansion House given by the Lord Mayor for the Merchants and Bankers of the City of London. Although we were bidden to wear full evening dress, our wives were not invited to dine with us. Instead, the wives of the principal speakers were given dinner separately and then, lo and behold, after dinner they were granted the great privilege of being permitted to sit in the Gallery to listen to their husbands' speeches! I doubt whether Jean found my observations on the money supply a source of unalloyed fascination.

The one banquet which I did enjoy was the annual gathering of the Overseas Bankers' Club in Guildhall. It had gradually developed into a very prestigious occasion and a significant proportion of the guests were leading bankers from overseas who would fly in specially for the dinner. I had spoken at the banquet when I was Chancellor, but now I was President of the Club and in that capacity it fell to me to invite two principal speakers. I decided that this was an occasion to use my influence, and I invited both Prince Charles and Mrs Thatcher. To my delight they both accepted. But it was not to be. Word came from No. 10 that they were very embarrassed because they ought to have realised that the Prime Minister could not make a politically controversial speech in the presence of the Heir to the Throne.

Prince Charles had taken a great deal of trouble in preparing his speech, which went down well. After all that has happened to the Royal Family in recent years, it is worth recalling that, as I talked with the Prince during that dinner, I remember thinking to myself what a dedicated and likeable man he was. The idea of forgoing the last remnants of privacy, of having laid bare even the most intimate details of one's personal life and being condemned to be 'on duty' for the rest of one's natural life would be, for me, almost a sentence of death. Many years ago, as Chancellor, I chaired the Select Committee to consider and update the Civil List. I recall a remark of the Queen's Private Secretary when he was giving evidence about her commitments. 'You and your colleagues in Parliament should remember that, unlike the Queen, you always have the option of retiring.'

25
Alaska

I have mentioned that, when I retired from politics, I wanted one full-time job, not a clutch of non-executive directorships. In fact, I made one exception. I accepted the unusual – indeed unique – position as a Government Director of British Petroleum. The story of BP is well known. Originally called the Anglo-Persian Oil Company, the British Government was for many years the largest shareholder and, by virtue of that, the Government was entitled to representation on the Board.

When I was appointed, in 1979, the Chairman of BP was Sir David Steel – the same David Steel who as a young solicitor used to brief me when I was at the Tax Bar. It was, I suppose, inevitable that some foreigners would assume that, with the British Government being the largest shareholder and with representation on the Board of Directors, the Company was subject to some form of political control. Nothing could be further from the truth. In the nine years I held the position, never once was there a problem on that score. Furthermore, although I was nominated by the Government, I always took the view that, in the event of a conflict, my overriding duty as a director was to consider the interests of the shareholders as a whole. Happily, no such conflict arose.

Because the bank had a presence in many of the countries where BP had an interest, I was able to make some minor contribution from time to time but, frankly, I do not think that I added much to the fortunes of BP. Nevertheless, being on the Board of one of the world's oil giants was certainly an interesting experience. The capital expenditure which had to be committed on any major new venture was enormous, but after having grappled with the nation's public finances, the figures were not difficult to absorb.

The history of the oil industry, and of BP in particular, is a truly epic tale, but I will ration myself to mentioning only one venture – Alaska. I was in Arizona on the bank's business and I had arranged to fly up to Anchorage to visit BP's oilfields on the North Slope of Alaska. As I was coming from a hot climate, I was concerned about the amount of clothing I thought I would have to carry to cope with temperatures on the North Slope which in winter are frequently minus 30 to minus 40 degrees Fahrenheit. With strong winds the chill factor is severe. I need not have concerned myself, because I was told that no ordinary clothing would be of any use, and that I would be completely kitted out when I arrived at Anchorage.

I should say here that most of my fellow non-executive directors who had visited the North Slope had done so in summer when the climate can be very pleasant. I chose to go in mid-winter for one simple reason. I wanted to get some idea of the working conditions at their most difficult. I was not disappointed; it was a truly remarkable experience. From Anchorage (where it was pretty cold) we flew some 600 miles north to Prudhoe Bay which is itself 250 miles north of the Arctic Circle. The Prudhoe Bay oilfield is the largest in North America and BP is the largest oil producer in Alaska. It had taken almost twenty years from the time when BP geologists first probed this remote part of the world to the day when the first oil flowed in 1977. For almost two months in the winter the sun never rises above the horizon. It is difficult to describe the working conditions. This is the land of the Eskimo and the grizzly bear, where some 2,000 men and women work through the winter in shifts twenty-four hours a day with never a glimpse of the sun, drilling for oil through 2,000 feet of permanently frozen ground or permafrost, and going down more than two miles to reach the oil reservoir.

What I found almost as impressive as the operations 'at the sharp end' was the back-up facilities for those who work on the North Slope – in addition to dining rooms and kitchens there are lounges, recreation areas, shops, a cinema and a library. Food was available twenty-four hours a day and somewhat to my surprise I was told that ice-cream was particularly popular! Once inside the buildings it was difficult to appreciate that just outside it was pitch black, day in, day out, and that if you were to step out without protection for only a few minutes you would be risking frostbite.

Here was a team of men and women grappling with the elements in what must surely be one of the most inhospitable terrains in the world. While other countries proclaim their successes from the rooftops, all too often we tend to underplay our achievements. Modesty can be an attractive attribute, but it can also be carried too far. Who would have thought, only two or three generations ago, that we would now be harvesting oil from beneath the North Sea, despite the tempestuous conditions which sometimes prevail?

Think of the nature of the man who goes out in search of oil which may not be produced in commercial quantities for almost a quarter of a century. And think of the foresight of the Board of Directors which authorises the capital expenditure involved in a venture which may fail and which, even if it succeeds, may not yield commercial results until most of the members of the Board have retired. To my mind the extraction of oil from Alaska and the North Sea is one of the wonders of the modern world.

26

Nelson Mandela

I have already mentioned that, after I retired from the House of Commons, I resolved not to get involved publicly in party political controversy. The reason was, quite simply, that there seemed to me to be something unseemly in a politician who had retired and acquired a lucrative position outside politics immediately turning round and starting to criticise his successor. Of course it was easy for me to take that line because I was fully occupied with my new responsibilities at the bank. If I had been languishing in retirement I would no doubt have been so frustrated that I might even have started writing letters to *The Times*. However, having eschewed becoming involved with party politics did not mean that I should not take part in major missions or Committees of Inquiry of one kind or another.

There were three which were particularly interesting. They concerned South Africa, the Falklands and China.

First, South Africa. Arrangements had been made for me to visit Nelson Mandela in Pollsmoor Prison. Shortly before I was due to go he sent this message to me: 'Tell Lord Barber that I am pleased that he is a member of the Commonwealth Group because that will give some reassurance to the whites.' The thought behind that simple message from a man who had been imprisoned by the whites for more than twenty years is a measure of his stature and a testament to his generosity of spirit.

The visit came about in this way. In October 1985 the Commonwealth Heads of Government had met in Nassau. The dominant subject under discussion was the situation in South Africa and, inevitably, there was much pressure to increase sanctions against that country. In the end it was decided to defer further consideration for six months, after which there would be another meeting to consider progress. Meanwhile, there was to be established a group of seven so-called 'Eminent Persons' who, within the allotted time of six months, were to attempt to initiate a 'process of dialogue across lines of colour, politics and religion, with a view to establishing a non-racial representative Government'.

Margaret Thatcher asked me to be her nominated member of the group. At first I declined. It seemed to me that, in the eyes of some, I would seem to be an inappropriate choice because, among other reasons, the Standard Chartered Bank had the controlling interest in the largest bank in South Africa and I was on the South African Board. Furthermore, because of my long-standing political association with Margaret and the Conservative Party, I would be portrayed as being there simply to do her bidding. In the end I was persuaded because of the experience which I had of the situations in both South Africa and the countries of black Africa south of the Sahara.

The other members of the group were Malcolm Fraser (former Prime Minister of Australia), General Obasanjo (former Head of the Federal Military Government of Nigeria), Dame Nita Barrow (President of the World Council of Churches), John Malecela (former Foreign Minister of Tanzania), Swaran Singh (former Minister of External Affairs in India) and Archbishop Edward Scott (Primate of the Anglican Church of Canada). The co-Chairmen were the two most senior members, Malcolm Fraser and General Obasanjo. Considering the composition of the group there were many in South Africa who assumed that the mission would never get off the ground, because it would not be allowed into the country. I must admit that the background of some of the members of the group made me wonder how they would look upon me – a Tory peer and a banker with financial interests in South Africa. In the event, any suspicion was soon dissipated and we worked as a team with complete trust.

One of the things which used to infuriate the South African Government was the way in which prominent visitors – Senator Kennedy was one such – would arrive in South Africa purporting to be on a fact-finding mission, only to voice their preconceived notions on arrival. I was therefore particularly interested when I heard of a suggestion that the group might agree that none of us would make a statement before our mission was complete. I should mention here that, although I never hesitated to express my abhorrence of apartheid, and to do so publicly in South Africa, I had always been on good terms with the South African authorities because I liked to think that I was always fair in recognising the reality of the situation. Who was it who said that to every complex problem there is an answer which is short, simple and wrong?

I then had an idea. Before the group had even met, I flew out to Johannesburg, ostensibly on business, having sent a message beforehand to the effect that if anyone in authority would like to meet me to discuss the EPG (as the Eminent Persons Group had become known) I would be available. When I landed at Johannesburg there was a message saying that the State President would like to meet me at Pretoria the following morning. And so I spent an hour with the President, P. W. Botha, the Foreign Minister, Pik Botha, and the Minister for Constitutional Development, Chris Huenis. They were clearly impressed by two factors. First, they regarded Margaret Thatcher as one of the few leaders who really understood the situation in South Africa and they knew that she was pressing hard for the visit to be accepted. Secondly, they were very taken with the idea that the group might give an undertaking not to make any statement until the mission had been completed.

The upshot was that we were accepted. Because we were likely to engage in a fair amount of shuttle diplomacy, particularly between the South African Government and the ANC in Lusaka, the Prime Minister of Canada had lent us a Canadian Air Force executive jet and I found myself travelling out to South Africa with Archbishop Scott. When lunch was about to be served I inquired of the steward whether we might have a drink. He explained that alcohol was not served on Canadian military aircraft. I asked him whether in future we could bring our own. He replied that there was no objection to that, whereupon I produced from my travel bag two miniature bottles of Scotch whisky and offered one to the Archbishop. His riposte was to produce from his bag a miniature bottle of Canadian rye. Thereafter we became close friends. He was in every way a man to be admired.

We visited all the Front Line States, had long discussions with the ANC, had twenty-one meetings with South African Government ministers and eventually produced what we called 'a possible negotiating concept'. It was deliberately couched in terms which were reasonable and moderate. Four years later Douglas Hurd, then Foreign Secretary, said this: 'We believe that the negotiating concept put forward by the Eminent Persons' Group remains the best basis on which to get negotiations underway. We are commending it to all parties in the dispute, including the South African Government and the ANC.'

What the so-called 'negotiating concept' did was to concentrate minds on the essentials of a lasting solution to the South African problem. Because of its significance in the long haul to freedom and democracy in South Africa, it merits being set out in full:

The South African Government has declared its commitment to dismantling the system of apartheid, to ending racial discrimination and to broad-based negotiations leading to new constitutional arrangements for power-sharing by all the people of South Africa. In the light of preliminary and as yet incomplete discussions with representatives of various organisations and groups, within and outside South Africa, we believe that in the context of specific and meaningful steps being taken towards ending apartheid, the following additional action might ensure negotiations and a break in the cycle of violence.

On the part of the Government: (a) Removal of the military from the townships, providing for freedom of assembly and discussion and suspension of detention without trial. (b) The release of Nelson Mandela and other political prisoners and detainees. (c) The unbanning of the ANC and PAC and the permitting of normal political activity.

On the part of the ANC and others: Entering negotiations and suspending violence.

It is our view that simultaneous announcements incorporating these ideas might be negotiated if the Government were to be interested in pursuing this broad approach.

In the light of the Government's indication to us that it: (i) is not in principle against the release of Nelson Mandela and similar prisoners; (ii) is not opposed in principle to the unbanning of any organisations; (iii) is prepared to enter into negotiations with the acknowledged leaders of the people of South Africa; (iv) is committed to removal of discrimination, not only from the statute books but also from South African society as a whole; (v) is committed to ending of white domination; (vi) will not prescribe who may represent black communities in negotiations on a new constitution for South Africa; (vii) is prepared to negotiate on an open agenda; the

South African Government may wish to give serious consideration to the approach outlined in this note.

We left the 'negotiating concept' with the Government for two
months and, although we were still meeting South African ministers from time to time, the Government neither accepted it nor
rejected it.

We then had our second meeting with Mandela. It was a long
meeting lasting over two hours. I wanted particularly to get his
personal reaction to the 'negotiating concept', which, of course, he
had not seen until then; bearing in mind that, if he were to accept it,
it would have involved a definite commitment to negotiations and,
quite clearly, would have involved a suspension of violence during
those negotiations. I wanted to know whether he personally could
accept it, but I was also very conscious of the fact that he had been
in prison for well over twenty years, and I knew that our conversation was not private. Indeed, there was no pretence of its being so.

I therefore started by saying to him: 'Before you answer and give
your views, I should point out that it has already been with the
South African Government for two months and they have not yet
reacted.' I therefore told him that as far as I was concerned I would
fully understand if he did not wish to comment at that stage but
would like to take more time to consider the proposals. He read
the paper carefully once through and he gave his answer without
hesitation. While he could not speak for the ANC, as far as he
personally was concerned he would accept the concept as a starting
point.

How easy it would have been for him to say that he must consult
his colleagues in the ANC before committing himself but, no, he
forthrightly said that he personally would accept it. This seemed to
me to show remarkable self-confidence in one who had been imprisoned for so long. I found Mandela to be a truly remarkable man
– intelligent, articulate, and with an authoritative presence. He was
also a man with a sense of humour.

Of course he hungered to be free and to be back again with his
family, but not at any price. He was not prepared to abandon those
who had suffered and died for the cause in which he believed. At a
time when there must have seemed little prospect of gaining his
freedom, here was a truly great man who, after nearly a quarter of a
century a political prisoner, had this to say to his people.

I cherish my own freedom dearly, but I care even more for your freedom. Too many have died since I went to prison. Too many have suffered for the love of freedom. I owe it to their widows, to their orphans, to their mothers and their fathers who have grieved and wept for them.

Not only have I suffered during these long lonely wasted years. I am no less life-loving than you are. But I cannot sell the birthright of the people to be free.

Only free men can negotiate. Prisoners cannot enter into contracts. Your freedom and mine cannot be separated.

After that second meeting with Mandela, we returned to Lusaka for a meeting with the ANC which lasted for more than six hours. We had every reason to believe that we were making real progress. Then we flew back to Cape Town, to the seat of Government, for our final meeting with the eight senior ministers who comprised the Constitutional Committee. They were the Minister for Constitutional Development and Planning, the Minister for Foreign Affairs, the Minister of National Education, the Minister of Law and Order, the Minister of Co-operation and Development, the Minister of Finance, the Minister of Home Affairs and the Minister of Justice. With the exception of the State President, this was the most powerful and influential group of ministers, and I was very conscious of the crucial importance of this last meeting.

There is no doubt that we were taken seriously by the South African Government. After all, we had already had twenty-one meetings with ministers. No previous mission had enjoyed such a reception and part of the reason for this was the fact that throughout the many months of discussion with South African ministers and the ANC we had kept our word and never once spoken to the press, either on or off the record. The purpose of the meeting with the Constitutional Committee was for them to report to and advise the State President. It was our last chance.

As we were assembling in the hotel before leaving for the meeting, we were informed of a dramatic development. It had just been announced on the radio that the South African Defence Forces had carried out raids on ANC bases in Zimbabwe, Botswana and Zambia. This was an act of extreme provocation only hours before the scheduled meeting. Remember that, in addition to Margaret Thatcher, the Presidents of Zimbabwe and Zambia had been responsible for the composition of the group. The kneejerk reaction of some was to call off the meeting in protest. Had we done so, I have no doubt that, despite the provocation, we would have been blamed by the South African authorities for breaking off the talks. The wise course was surely to attend the meeting and to make no mention of the raids at all. There was too much at stake to risk being wrong-footed at that stage. So we arrived at the meeting and, as we had agreed, not even a passing reference was made to the raids.

Before I recount what transpired at the meeting, it provided me with a striking instance of how misleading first appearances can be. Placed almost directly opposite me was F. W. de Klerk, who was then Minister of National Education. He sat sullen and silent during the long meeting. I do not recollect him uttering one word. I took an instant dislike to the man because I interpreted his studied silence to imply that he viewed the whole exercise as a waste of time. Now, after all that has happened since, I suspect that the architect of South Africa's democracy remained silent not because he disagreed with what we were saying, but because he approved of it and, at that stage, was naturally hesitant to express his views openly in front of his ministerial colleagues.

The discussion soon turned once again to the issue of violence – should the South African Government accept an undertaking from the ANC to suspend violence during negotiations, as we had suggested; or, as a condition of starting negotiations, should they insist on the renunciation of violence for all time? The Government's view was clearly expressed in a letter ten days later from Pik Botha, the Foreign Minister: 'The South African Government cannot accept the suggestion that violence should be discontinued only for so long as negotiations take place. To use violence or the threat of violence as a bargaining counter is unacceptable to the South African Government.'

It may be thought that there is here a parallel with the approach of the British Government to developments in Northern Ireland, but any similarity is only superficial. In Northern Ireland there is an established democracy with universal suffrage. Every law-abiding citizen has political rights and is entitled to the protection of the law. There is freedom of speech. In such a situation it is wholly reasonable to insist on the complete renunciation of violence for all time by any group which wishes to enter into negotiations with the

Government. In South Africa at the time of our meetings the situation was completely different. Those who were represented by the ANC had no democratic means of pursuing their objectives and, in those circumstances, we thought that the proposal to suspend violence was reasonable.

At the end of the meeting we parted amicably and returned to London to await a formal response from the South African Government.

By now our six months were almost up and, sadly, we failed in our immediate task. I have no doubt that several senior South African ministers, including in particular Pik Botha, the Minister for Foreign Affairs, believed that our approach was the right one. The others, under the reactionary oversight of the then State President, P. W. Botha, simply could not bring themselves to take what to them seemed to be a leap into the unknown. But I do not think our mission was in vain. In the years that followed the British Government took the view that what we were proposing offered the best chance of success.

We returned home to write our Report. Clearly it was highly desirable that, if at all possible, our Report should be unanimous. At the eleventh hour I found myself in direct disagreement with the other six members of the group. Our mandate, which I have quoted, did not include the matter of sanctions. That was something not for us but for the Heads of Government, and in any event I was personally opposed to further sanctions. Yet the other members of the group wished to include the following passage in our Report: 'When one examines alternatives and options, further economic measures do in fact represent the only alternatives remaining. Diplomatic persuasion has patently failed. There is no reason to believe it would be any more effective in the future. Such measures would need to be substantive and considerable.'

I was determined to stand firm. We were due to have our final meeting on a Saturday afternoon. We had to settle all outstanding questions at that meeting because most of the members of the group had made arrangements to return to their respective countries that weekend. I decided to contact the two co-Chairmen (Malcolm Fraser and General Obasanjo) that morning to warn them that if they would not excise the offending passage I would have to include a minority Report. To my surprise, Malcolm Fraser could not be found, so I telephoned General Obasanjo and was on my way through Hyde Park to the Grosvenor House Hotel where he was staying when my car phone rang: 'This is 10 Downing Street. The Lord Privy Seal would like to speak to Lord Barber.' My driver pulled up and left the car and on the telephone came Willie Whitelaw. To my absolute astonishment, it appeared that Malcolm Fraser had travelled by car all the way up to Cumbria to ask Willie to intervene to persuade me to go along with the Report as drafted. Needless to say, his journey was a waste of time. The offending words did not appear in the final version and happily we were able to produce a unanimous Report which undoubtedly contributed to its influence.

At the time I was meeting Mandela, his wife, Winnie, was still a power in the land and, without doubt, a woman with considerable charisma. I should stress that this was before she was accused of being involved with the death of one of her young followers and before she had made her inflammatory remarks about 'necklacing'. It should also be borne in mind that, year after year in very difficult circumstances, she had stood by her husband and certainly over that long period her constant and unfailing support had been a comfort to him. I mention these factors because at that time she was a person of some consequence and, because of this, it was right that we should see her. On one such occasion she was given permission to meet us for coffee at a small restaurant called 'Thatches'. One of our group could not resist the temptation to have me pose with her with the name of the restaurant prominently in the background. In the light of her more recent antics I would not be so accommodating today!

I have said that she had to obtain permission to meet us. This was because, at the time of our visits, she was the subject of banning orders. I still have a copy of those Orders which were operative for five years. It is impossible to exaggerate the all-embracing nature of the restrictions. Issued under the hand of the Minister of Law and Order, they ran to more than 1,000 words, of which I will quote less than 100 as an illustration of their draconian attack on the most basic liberties:

I hereby prohibit you from attending within the Republic of South Africa any gathering as contemplated in sub-paragraph (ii) of the said Section 20, of the nature, class or kind set out below: (a) any social gathering, that is to say, any gathering at which the persons present also have social intercourse with one another; (b) any political gathering, that is to say, any gathering at which any form of State or any principle or policy of the Government of a State is propagated, defended, attacked, criticised or discussed.

A postscript. Towards the end of our mission I was telephoned by Nelson Mandela's lawyer, Ismael Ayob. He asked to see me to convey a message from Mrs Mandela. He duly arrived to tell me that she believed that if only she could meet Mrs Thatcher they could together make real progress towards a peaceful solution for South Africa. They could meet secretly in Botswana. That was one approach which we did not follow up.

27

The Falklands

I said that there were three major missions or Committees of Inquiry in which I took part after I retired from politics. The second concerned the Falklands.

On Christmas Eve 1982, eight years after I had left the House of Commons, I was relaxing at home in Yorkshire when Michael Jopling, the Government Chief Whip, telephoned and said that the Prime Minister had asked him to come over to see me that day. Why should the Government Chief Whip want to see me on Christmas Eve? The reason will become apparent when I explain what led up to this visit.

From time to time in political life allegations and accusations are made which one knows to be false. But once the allegations are made, sometimes under the protection of Parliamentary privilege, they tend to stick 'No smoke without fire'. In most cases it is simply annoying or hurtful and one has to accept it as part of the price to pay for entering politics in the first place. But when what is alleged is sufficiently serious or impinges upon responsibility for matters of life and death, a formal investigation is essential. One means of searching out the truth is to set up, with all-party agreement, a small committee of Privy Councillors to inquire and report.

Such was the case with the Falkland Islands Review. There were six of us, two Conservative (Lord Watkinson and myself), two Labour (Lord Lever of Manchester and Merlyn Rees MP), one retired Permanent Secretary (Sir Patrick Nairne) and a Chairman of unparalleled experience (Lord Franks). Not many men have been British Ambassador to Washington, the head of two Oxford colleges, Chairman of one of our biggest High Street banks and declined the invitation to become Governor of the Bank of England. That was Lord Franks. The Committee was formed as a result of repeated allegations in Parliament and in the media that the secret intelligence available to the Government was such that the

Government was negligent in not having foreseen the Argentine invasion of the Falklands.

The full terms of reference were as follows: 'To review the way in which the responsibilities of Government in relation to the Falkland Islands and their Dependencies were discharged in the period leading up to the Argentine invasion of the Falkland Islands on 2 April 1982, taking account of all such factors in previous years as are relevant.'

We were provided with all the relevant papers that the Prime Minister personally saw, all the Cabinet papers, every report from the Intelligence Agencies bearing upon the matter and every assessment on Argentina and the Falklands made by the Joint Intelligence Organisation – and much else besides. Because of the sensitive nature of many of the documents, we were provided with our own suite of offices in the old Admiralty building. Also, because we would be inquiring into matters concerning the conduct of ministers and officials in the Foreign Office and the Ministry of Defence, our secretariat came from the Home Office.

At our first meeting Lord Franks led us into a room with a line of security cabinets which were packed with documents. We knew then the magnitude of the task before us. Nevertheless we agreed that, given the nature of our inquiry, it would not be satisfactory to rely on summaries, however accurate and comprehensive, and we also decided that we should read individually the various documents available to us. We therefore set aside the best part of the first two months solely to read the papers. We then had thirty-nine sessions where we took oral evidence, in private, from ministers and officials including the Prime Minister and three former Prime Ministers, and, of course, from the intelligence community. We also got in touch with the editors of the national and provincial newspapers asking whether they had any specific information which indicated the possibility of Argentine action against the Falkland Islands.

There are those who contend that it ought to have been possible to settle the Falklands dispute with the Argentine long ago, and there has been much discussion about the enormous amount of taxpayers' money which has been poured into the Falkland Islands since they were liberated. The events which occurred and the decisions which took place after the liberation were not, of course, within our terms of reference, but it is worth mentioning here one fundamental point. Because we live in a democracy, it is not simply a question of whether the expenditure is cost-effective, or even whether it is right or wrong. There may be fewer than 2,000 islanders, but the hard fact is that any proposal which they were not prepared to endorse would never get through the House of Commons.

There are cogent arguments in favour of a 'leasehold' solution. The idea is that the British Government would transfer the sovereignty of the islands to the Argentine with certain safeguards in perpetuity and a provision that the Argentine would lease back the islands to the United Kingdom for a period of years, which could be quite lengthy – maybe fifty years or more.

I always thought that there was much to be said for the proposal, but the islanders would not accept it and so, whatever might be the view of the Government of the day, the House of Commons would never approve a solution which was against the 'wishes' of the islanders. It is interesting to note how the choice of one word can make all the difference. The Argentine Government has always relied on the fact that the United Nations Resolutions referred to the 'interests' (rather than the 'wishes') of the islanders, and they reaffirmed the Argentine's intention of respecting those interests, including the preservation of the way of life and cultural traditions of the islanders. So I am afraid that the hard-pressed British tax-payer will have to continue to foot the bill.

From time to time during our inquiry I wondered what such a detailed and concentrated investigation of any period of mine at the Treasury would have thrown up. So often, with the benefit of hindsight, actions would have been different and comments might have been better left unsaid. Although we stated that we had taken particular care to avoid the exercise of hindsight in reaching judgements on the developments of policy and on the actions of ministers and officials, we did conclude that there were occasions when different decisions might have been taken, and where fuller consideration of alternative courses of action might have been advantageous.

Politicians learn the hard way that it is not enough merely to say the right thing. What matters is how the media will interpret it.

I was concerned about certain passages in our Report which, if taken out of context and in isolation, could give a false impression. Consider, for instance, the following passage, bearing in mind that the Argentine invasion of the Falklands took place on 2 April 1982.

Officials in both the Foreign and Commonwealth Office and the Ministry of Defence were looking to Ministers to review the outcome of the contingency planning they had done in view of a potentially more aggressive posture by Argentina. In the event, Government policy towards Argentina and the Falkland Islands was never formally discussed outside the Foreign and Commonwealth Office after January 1981. Thereafter, the time was never judged to be ripe although we were told in oral evidence that, subject to the availability of Ministers, a Defence Committee meeting could have been held at any time, if necessary at short notice. There was no meeting of the Defence Committee to discuss the Falklands until 1 April 1982; and there was no reference to the Falklands in Cabinet, even after the New York talks of 26 and 27 February, until Lord Carrington reported on events in South Georgia on 25 March 1982.

We cannot say what the outcome of a meeting of the Defence Committee might have been, or whether the course of events would have been altered if it had met in September 1981; but, in our view, it could have been advantageous, and fully in line with Whitehall practice, for ministers to have reviewed collectively at that time, or in the months immediately ahead, the current negotiating position; the implications of the conflict between the attitudes of the islanders and the aims of the Junta; and the longer-term policy options in relation to the dispute.

I was afraid that by expressing the opinion that it might have been advantageous if certain things had been done differently, the conclusion might have been drawn, either quite innocently or by those who were ill-disposed to the Government, that the invasion could have been prevented. This was not our view, and I was very insistent that this should be made crystal clear. We therefore included the following words: 'There is no reasonable basis for any suggestion – which would be purely hypothetical – that the invasion would have been prevented if the Government had acted in the ways indicated in our report.' Without those words I would have found it difficult not to express dissent.

The Review took six months and we reached the unanimous conclusion that the invasion could not have been foreseen by the

Government. What I found particularly fascinating was the way in which a truly thorough investigation, with unlimited access to papers and people, showed that so many of the assertions which had been made were wholly without foundation.

It had been asserted that the Government had clear warnings of the invasion from American Intelligence sources, including satellite sources. The fact was that the Government received no such intelligence. Newspaper reports claimed that only a week before the invasion the British Embassy in Buenos Aires had passed on definite information to London about an invasion and predicted the exact day. There was no truth in the reports. That is not to say that the journalists who filed those reports may not have done so in good faith. It was not our task to establish whether or not the journalists were told something to that effect. The allegation was clearly a serious one and it was our task to ascertain whether any such communication from our Embassy in Buenos Aires was in fact made. Having examined all the relevant telegrams and intelligence reports and interviewed the individuals concerned, we were satisfied that no such communication was made.

It was also claimed that the Government rejected advice from the Commander-in-Chief, Fleet, to send submarines a fortnight before the invasion. Again there was no foundation for the claim. Then there was the report that John Nott, Secretary of State for Defence, had seen Captain Barker, Captain of HMS *Endurance*, a survey ship in the Antarctic, and ignored his advice. In fact, they had never even met each other.

We ended our Report with these words:

> We conclude that we would not be justified in attaching any criticism or blame to the present Government for the Argentine Junta's decision to commit its act of unprovoked aggression in the invasion of the Falkland Islands on 2nd April 1982.

Suppose that we had found otherwise? Suppose that we had concluded that the Government had been negligent and that British soldiers had been killed needlessly as a result of that negligence? I do not believe that Margaret Thatcher could have survived. No wonder she sent her Chief Whip to see me on that Christmas Eve.

We were due to sign our Report seven days later, on New Year's Eve, and Margaret was concerned to know the outcome before Christmas. We had deliberated in strict secrecy for six months, and

I could not now disclose the contents of the Report before we had all signed it. However, it was the season of goodwill and I did not think it unreasonable to breach the confidentiality of our work to the extent of sending her a message telling her that she had every reason to enjoy her Christmas.

28

China

I come now to the third mission – to China. This came about partly because of my association with the bank, but also because of my experience in government. Because the Chartered Bank had been in China since the middle of the last century we were highly regarded by the Chinese authorities. We also earned high marks in their eyes for another reason. During the Cultural Revolution our senior manager in China, David Johnston, was arrested on a trumped-up charge and held in solitary confinement for the best part of a year. Unlike many of the foreign enterprises which packed up and left at the time of the Cultural Revolution, the Chartered Bank stayed on and, indeed, sent out a replacement manager. (Some years later when I was visiting the bank's office in Vancouver I had lunch with David Johnston. He was a very courageous man.)

I had visited China from time to time and I found that one thing that puzzled our European customers was that the bank in Beijing was referred to by the local Chinese as 'Makalee' Bank. The explanation was that one of our earliest expatriate managers was called John MacKellar. He obviously made a great impression and so what was originally known as MacKellar's Bank became with the passage of time Makalee Bank.

When I travelled around China for the Standard Chartered Bank the arrangements were made by the Bank of China, but it was after I left the bank that I had my two most memorable visits, involving discussions with Chairman Deng Xiaoping, Premier Li Peng, General Secretary Jiang Zemin and other leaders. I could not have had a more illuminating insight into the minds of the Chinese leaders.

I was one of a group of so-called 'international personalities' who were invited by the Chinese Government to Beijing for private meetings with the leading Chinese decision-makers. We stayed at the State Guest House. The subject of the first visit was 'China and the World in the 90s', and the first thing that struck me was the way in which their considered strategy stretched far into the future. Not for them any trimming of policies because of an impending General Election. Much is written about the obvious evils of authoritarian rule, but it has to be admitted that it does make it possible to plan for the longer term. It is also in the nature of the Chinese, with their long history, to think big and to think way ahead.

I can still see the diminutive Deng, smoking away with his spittoon as his feet, talking about the three stages of their development strategy. The first stage was to provide sufficient food and clothing for the Chinese people and that stage had been accomplished two years ahead of schedule. The second stage was to double the country's output by the year 2000 and to reach what Deng's translator described as 'a well-to-do living standard'. The third stage was to reach a level of output which was translated as being equivalent to the level of 'a middle developed country'. That stage they hoped to reach by the year of 2050.

But if their eyes were set on the middle of the twenty-first century, they were also grappling with the very real problems of the present. The key issue was how to get through the interim period when they were moving gradually from a centrally planned economy towards a socialist market economy. Even in the short decade or two during which I was visiting China, I saw for myself the dramatic social and economic changes which were taking place. The budding entrepreneur selling his goods by the roadside and hoping to make enough profit to buy his first bicycle. The striking change in people's dress which followed the arrival of choice. The Chinese are an industrious people and the leadership is harnessing that industry by encouraging individual enterprise and competition. When I jokingly said that what they were really doing was abandoning Socialism, they replied with a smile that what they were pursuing was 'Socialism with Chinese characteristics'.

My second invitation came shortly after the Tiananmen Square tragedy. Because of this, it was a particularly significant visit. My wife, Rosemary, came with me and, again, we stayed at the State Guest House. The general question of the relationship of economic liberalisation to political reform was very much in the minds of the Chinese leaders, as it was in my own. The country is enormous, both in size and in population, and with the rapid pace of modernisation it is inevitable that there should be severe strains. Yet if they are to achieve the improvement in material welfare, they have to maintain stability. The question is how fast can economic liberalisation proceed with the present political arrangements. It is all too easy for the West to call for radical political reforms, but he would be an irresponsible leader who would sacrifice the stability and unity of the country. There has to be a balance and I do not have much sympathy with those naive people who would put that stability at risk.

Because my second visit came shortly after Tiananmen Square, I took the opportunity on several occasions to point out that what had happened there had been seen all over the world, on millions of television sets, and had done incalculable harm to China's image. In particular, it made the British wonder what the future held for the people of Hong Kong. Somewhat to my surprise the Chinese showed no resentment at my raising the matter in pretty blunt terms. Indeed, I got the impression that they wanted to have the opportunity of putting their side of the case.

The frankest explanation came from Jiang Zemin, the General Secretary of the Central Committee of the Chinese Communist Party. He said, with engaging openness, that all politicians sometimes made mistakes, and that they had made one big mistake. They had dithered and allowed the demonstration to continue for too long. If they had called a halt after a week or two, the demonstration could have been ended peacefully without bloodshed. But then, having made the mistake of allowing the demonstration to continue and to gain momentum, they lost control. They had no riot aids such as water cannon or rubber bullets and he pointed out that, whereas the British authorities were used to dealing with unruly demonstrations, they were not!

What happened in Tiananmen Square cannot be justified, but it is not unreasonable to ask this question: having made the initial mistake of allowing the demonstration to grow and to get out of hand, and believing that, unless halted, it would spread to other parts of China and that the consequent turmoil could put in jeopardy the whole of the reform programme and that, at that stage, only a show of overwhelming force could stop it, was it so unreasonable to believe that the mere threat of tanks might have caused the crowd to disperse without those tragic deaths?

One surprise. Jiang Zemin is one of the most powerful men in China and, just before we parted, he added for good measure: 'I know what I am talking about because at the height of the trouble I dressed up as a painter and went into Tiananmen Square to see the situation for myself and, although I mingled with the crowd, nobody recognised me.'

I have one very special memento of my first visit to China. It was early in 1978 and I was staying in a government guest house in Kweilin, which is set among some of the most picturesque and romantic scenery in all China. Our flight was delayed but we were quite happy to spend an extra unscheduled night in this fascinating part of China. On the day before I had noticed a man painting a large mural in one of the communal rooms. The following evening, when we should already have left, he was in the hall completing a painting of lotus flowers. I had time on my hands and I watched him for half an hour or so.

A young Chinese man who was also there introduced himself and told me that he was from Hong Kong and married to the painter's daughter. He said that his father-in-law knew who I was and wondered why I was so interested in his painting. I made some polite answer about technique and the son-in-law said something in Chinese. The young man then told me that, when the painting was finished, his father-in-law would like to present it to me as a mark of goodwill between our two countries. I made another little speech which was duly translated.

The young man then went on to say that I was very honoured because his father-in-law did not sell his paintings. He was paid by the State and he either painted for the State or occasionally gave a painting to one of his friends. As I watched the painting develop, with its bold brush strokes, it was obvious that it could only have been painted by a Chinese. Yet there was something quite different from the traditional Chinese flower painting. There was a distinct touch of Western influence. I began to realise that this was not one of those embarrassing occasions when courtesy demanded that I should accept a gift which I did not want. As the painting neared completion I was becoming quite excited, but I could not have anticipated the conversation which followed.

The young man asked me: 'Do you know who my father-in-law is?' I replied that I did not. He said: 'He is probably the most famous painter in China today.' I accepted the claim with a pinch of salt but made a suitable reply. He then asked: 'Have you seen the huge tapestry behind the statue of Chairman Mao at the entrance to the Memorial Hall in Tiananmen Square?' I had indeed seen it. 'Well,' said the young man, 'my father-in-law designed it.' He then added for good measure: 'If you want to see some more of my father-in-law's work, you will find five pages of it in the *Sunday Times* colour supplement of two weeks ago.' I still have that colour supplement. I had the painting framed in a simple black lacquer frame.

Shortly afterwards an elderly Hong Kong Chinese was having dinner with me in London and I showed him the painting. He liked it but in his view the frame was not right. In his broken English he said: 'It is like me coming to dinner in a black tie but wearing tennis shoes.' So he took the measurements and before long there arrived a fine rosewood frame specially made in China. The painting by Huang Yung-Yu still has an honoured place in my drawing room.

I had always been fascinated by the Far East and South East Asia and, several years before those memorable visits to China, I travelled to Saigon at a time when the Vietnam War was at its height. The Vietcong had deployed anti-aircraft guns close to Saigon and, because of this, it was too dangerous to attempt a normal approach to the runway. Instead we flew directly over the airfield and 'spiralled' down to a safe landing.

The first thing that struck me was the lasting influence of the French in this part of Indo-China. The Vietnamese women not only had a natural beauty, but in their dress and their bearing they manifested an elegance which I could not help contrasting with the sickening cruelty which was taking place in that country. I am referring not to modern weapons of mass destruction, but to the individual torture of one person by another and the human degradation which was all part of that truly nasty war.

We were briefed by General Westmoreland and others, but my purpose in recounting this visit is not to comment on the war but to introduce the Air Attaché, Wing Commander Helmore, with whom I stayed. To say that he was no ordinary Air Attaché would be a serious understatement. In the evening he insisted on taking us on a tour of the Saigon night spots and then, despite the curfew (which he assured us did not apply to him), he rowed us out to a yacht which was moored in the Mekong River. There we sat drinking beer to the sound of distant gunfire.

The following morning he flew us over territory held by the Vietcong and, much as I enjoy the thrill of low flying, I could not help thinking, as he was weaving around just above the treetops, that we were perhaps somewhat unnecessarily low to be over Vietcong territory. Wing Commander Helmore was certainly an engaging character. Sadly, the last I heard of him was that he had drowned in the Bay of Biscay.

Envoi

It is seven years since I married Rosemary, without whose encouragement and, indeed, perseverance these reminiscences would never have appeared. We and our parents had known each other for many years, but we then lost touch. By the time we married I had already retired from the bank and we have therefore had much time to spend together. Between us we have two sons and three daughters, not to mention the grandchildren. Perhaps it is because we were both brought up in the same Yorkshire environment that, despite many years apart, we have so much in common. We have so many similar tastes – from music and travel to *Coronation Street*! We both like to go back to Yorkshire, although we no longer have any family there. Rosemary's love of racing is something she inherited from her father, a respected canon of the Church of England, whom I remember as a keen follower of the Turf. It was only since we were married that Rosemary confided in me that when his parishioners thought that he was going for a well-earned rest at Scarborough he was in fact on his way to Monte Carlo to play the tables.

I can understand those who, after one happy marriage, prefer henceforth to lead a single life, but life for me would be a barren affair without someone to share its joys and tribulations. I have never been one to wear my heart on my sleeve, and I am not now to be tempted otherwise. I will simply say that, when I met Rosemary again, fortune certainly smiled on me.

I am now seventy-six and, as I look back, I am grateful to have had such an eventful and varied life. Disappointments and sadness there have been, but they have been more than matched by excitement, happiness and good fortune. We cannot always determine the course of events, but as new situations develop so new opportunities arise and it is up to each one of us to make the best of those new opportunities. That is what I have always tried to do.

Index